Generative Analysis

A Second Course

Generative Analysis

A Second Course

Jeong-Seok Kim

SEJIN

Preface

Two and a half years have passed since my first course on syntax, *Syntactic Analysis*, was published in 2012. I hope the book has inspired more students to study syntax. Now I am happy to announce that my second course on syntax, *Generative Analysis*, is being published. The contents of this book stemmed from the lecture notes for an introductory course for graduate students, taught at Korea University for many years. I hope that readers will use this helpful book to embark on further in-depth study of syntax.

This book has two main goals. The first is to provide a general level introduction to syntax while providing key concepts on the specific level as evidenced by the research of the past 60 years. The second is to build a bridge linking generative territories between the Principles-and-Parameters theory and the Minimalist Program. My discussion is mainly focused on English, minimizing digressions on other languages unless deemed necessary.

To achieve these goals, the book is comprised of three components. First, I provide a comprehensive overview of Generative Grammar in terms of where it stands today, paying particular attention to key concepts. This brief synopsis of the generative enterprise will give readers the foundation they need to engage in the rest of the book. Second, I provide exercises through which students can evoke their critical thinking skills by writing short essays. The exercises enable readers to foster syntactic argumentation and are explicitly designed to deepen students' understanding of syntactic patterns through reasoning. Third, I often resort to labeled bracket notation of phrase markers instead of drawing standard two-dimensional tree diagrams. Students who wish to master full-fledged tree diagrams should refer to my first course book. The margins to the left or right of the main text are meant to provide space for practicing trees.

The target audience for the book is advanced undergraduate students or first-year graduate students. Although prior knowledge of advanced syntax is not a prerequisite, I acknowledge that some background knowledge of syntax is indispensible. There are many textbooks and handbooks that can be used to fill any gaps in schema. Of course, my first course on syntax, *Syntactic Analysis*, is strongly recommended.

This book is organized as follows: Chapter 1 presents the classical generative architecture of Universal Grammar before the advent of the Minimalist Program. The successive chapters from Chapter 2 to Chapter 10 discuss the seven modules of the Principles-and-Parameters theory including the nature of Move α and Logical Form: X'-theory, θ-theory, Government theory, Bounding theory, Case theory, Binding theory, and Control theory. Sometimes, I hint at the minimalist solution to the unresolved problems of the Principles-and-Parameters theory. Currently, the Minimalist Program prevails and is making great strides in changing the face of Universal Grammar. In this light, the last two chapters provide a simple and sharp outline of the ongoing development of the linguistic adventure called *Minimalism*. Chapter 11 introduces the basic minimalist tools that duplicate the remarkable feats of strength Transformational Generative Grammar has accomplished. Chapter 12 deals with the more recent trend of Minimalism, covering Cyclic Spell-Out, Locality, Agree, and Feature-Inheritance.

Many people have contributed to Part II of my 'Generative Grammar trilogy' in their own ways. The current book would not have been possible without the help of my colleagues who have used *Syntactic Analysis: A First Course* of this trilogy project: Sang-Gu Kang (Korea University), Youngjun Jang (Chung-Ang University), Il-Kon Kim (Hanyang University), Keun-hee Lee (Andong National University), Wooseung Lee (Konkuk University), Myung Ki Oh (Kangwon University), Mean-Young Song (Dongguk University), and Byoung-seon Yang (Jeonju University). The scores of students at Korea University and elsewhere and their positive and negative responses have prodded me to pursue this book. Special thanks go to my students for their devotion: Eun-Kyoung Bae, Da-eun Chang, A Ram Jo, Duk-Ho Jung, Mi-ju Jung, Hye-ri Kim, Yunhui Kim, Kyung Mi Lee, BoKyeog Park, Myung Hoon Park, Beo Deul Song, and Hye Jin Yang. I am deeply indebted to Duk-Ho Jung for his help in preparing the manuscript and reading earlier drafts. Lastly, I would like to express my gratitude to Professor Ho-min Sohn who extended an invitation to me so I could spend my sabbatical leave at the Center for Korean Studies at the University of Hawaii, Manoa and to the Center Director Sang-Hyop Lee for providing me with an office and an optimal research environment.

As always, my wife and two daughters have been a great source of support and encouragement throughout the writing of this book and during my one year stay at the University of Hawaii, Manoa. This book is thus dedicated to Eun-Young, Yijun (Henry J. Kaiser High School), and Yijae (Niu Valley Middle School).

Jeong-Seok Kim
Center for Korean Studies
University of Hawaii at Manoa

July 2014

Contents

1 Generative Architecture

We couldn't start from scratch. The reader requires some background in syntax (see Kim 2012).

We have a mechanism in our **mind/brain** that assigns structure to sequences of words. This mechanism is called **Grammar**.

This book aims to provide a solid background of the Principles-and-Parameters (**P&P**) approach and a quick review of the **minimalist** approach to **Generative Grammar**.

1.1 Universal Grammar

One of the main research topics in modern generative linguistics since the mid-1950s is the so-called **Plato's Problem**.

(1) How are children able to acquire grammatical **competence** despite the **impoverished** nature of the data that is input to this process?

Children are **biologically** equipped with Universal Grammar (**UG**). UG is composed of principles with **open parameter values** which are set by **experience**, i.e., the primary linguistic data (**PLD**). **Principles** are what is invariant across languages. **Parameters** are what varies across languages. UG is proposed to answer Plato's Problem (i.e., the **ease of acquisition**).

Cross-linguistic exploration suggests that syntax is partly invariant across humans and partly subject to parametric variation.

Particular Grammar (**PG**) is the output of setting open parameter values of UG in response to the properties of the PLD. That is, exposure to the PLD **triggers** UG to change into PG.

(2)

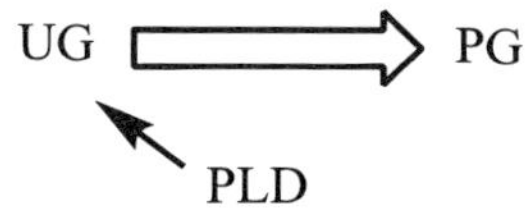

Government and Binding (**GB**) Theory is a very successful theory of Grammar. GB is the most theoretically and empirically developed version of a P&P approach to UG.

Sentences (or clauses) have the following basic properties (Hornstein et al. 2005):

(3) a. Sentences are **elementary linguistic units**.
b. **Sounds** (or signs) and **meanings** are paired via sentences.
c. Sentences are **hierarchically** composed of small expressions.
d. Sentences may have **displacement** effects in that one expression occupies two or more different positions.
e. Sentences may be **recursive**.

1.2 Generative Models

Grammar has a T-type organization. GB assumes four levels as in (4): DS, SS, PF, and LF.

(4) **T-model** = Y-model = Inverted Y-model

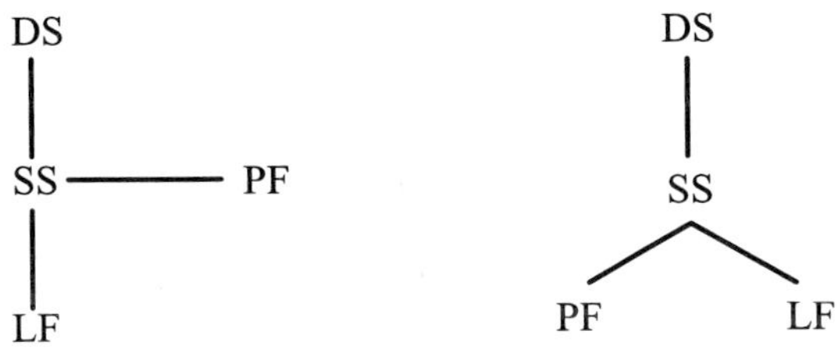

D-structure (**DS**) provides a structural description of lexical strings, following the principles of phrase structure and argument structure. Pure GF-θ is represented at DS. There is one-to-one correspondence between grammatical function (**GF**) and θ-role.

In GB, DS is the **starting point** for a derivation. It is the **output** of phrase structure operations plus lexical insertion, and it is the **input** to the transformational operations.

S-structure (**SS**) is related to DS via the application of movement transformations (substitution and adjunction).♣ SS is also related to Phonetic Form (PF) and Logical Form (LF). SS is the point at which the derivation **splits**, sending off one copy to PF and one copy to LF. Several grammatical modules such as those in (5) apply at SS. It is the **most theory-internal** level.

(5)
a. Case
b. Some aspects of Binding
c. Some aspects of the Empty Category Principle (ECP)
d. Subjacency
e. Certain Parameters: Wh-Parameter, V-raising Parameter, etc.

LF is derived from SS via invisible movement operations. LF is an interface level. The following grammatical modules apply at LF.

♣ See chapter 4 for the discussion of substitution and adjunction.

(6) a. The ECP
b. Binding
c. Control

PF is derived from SS via the application of phonological rules. PF is an interface level. It is very unlikely that any syntactic rule can apply at the PF level of representation, which is not a phrase marker. Syntactic rules may apply during the derivation from SS to PF, as long as syntactic structures are still available.♣

Move is an operation. It can be either **overt** or **covert**. The following illustrates some of covert movement operations. (The solid line indicates overt movement, and the dotted line covert movement.)

(7) (Covert) wh-movement
a. Who saw what?
b. [$_{CP}$ who$_1$-what$_2$ [$_{IP}$ t$_1$ saw t$_2$]] or
c. [$_{CP}$ what$_2$-who$_1$ [$_{IP}$ t$_1$ saw t$_2$]]

(8) Expletive-Associate constructions
a. There is a man in the garden.
b. [there-a man$_1$ is t$_1$ in the garden]

(cf. Chomsky *KL*)

(9) Anaphor raising
a. Steve saw himself in the mirror.
b. [Steve INFL-himself$_1$ see t$_1$ in the mirror]

(cf. Chomsky *KL*)

♣ Phrase marker is two-dimensional, thus having structure as well as linear sequence. PF level is one-dimensional, thus having only linearity.

In (7) *who* moves overtly to Spec(ifier) of CP, and *what* moves covertly and adjoins to Spec of CP. In (8) the associate moves covertly and adjoins to the expletive for Case. In (9) the anaphor moves covertly and adjoins to INFL in order to be licensed by the antecedent.

The **Projection Principle** in (10) makes derivations **monotonic**.

(10) The Projection Principle
Lexical information must be preserved at every **syntactic level** such as DS, SS, and LF.

As a consequence, a **trace** is required to preserve the thematic and structural information encoded at DS. The Projection Principle forces each movement to leave a trace.

GB has a very simple transformational component, which includes two rules.

(11) a. Bind: It allows free indexing of nominals.
b. Move: It allows anything to move anywhere anytime.

In GB, **Government Theory** is a fundamental module.♣ It is involved in several modules such as Case Theory, θ-theory, Binding Theory, or Bounding Theory.

(12) a. Case is assigned under government.
b. θ-roles are assigned under government.
c. Binding domains are defined via governors.
d. The ECP and Subjacency are stated in terms of barriers, which are defined via government.

The following is an articulated version of (4). (The solid arrow indicates that relevant rules or modules directly impact on a level. The dotted arrow indicates that the impact of relevant rules or modules on a level is somewhat controversial.)

♣ A module is one of several separate parts that can be combined to form a larger object, such as a machine or building.

(13)

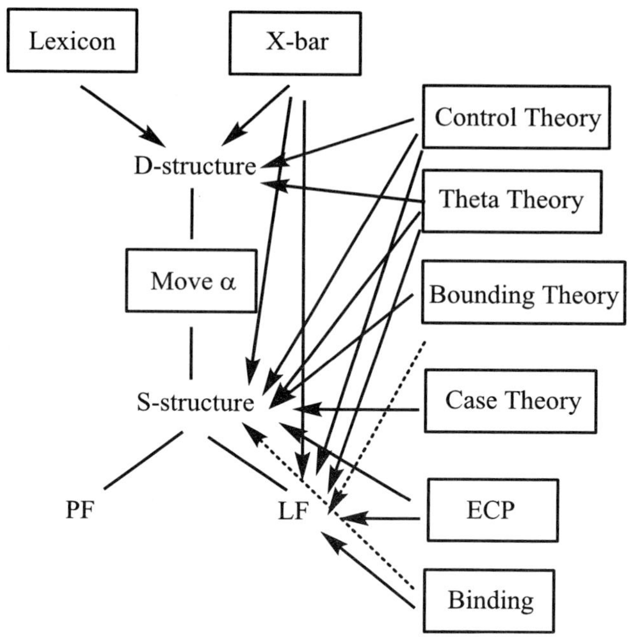

The **Transformational Component** has **overgeneration** problems. To compensate, several modules are proposed.

(14) **GB Modules**

a. X'-theory
The X'-schema (at DS, SS, and LF)

b. Control Theory
The PRO Theorem (at DS, SS, and LF)

c. θ-theory
The θ-criterion (at DS, SS, and LF)
The Projection Principle (at DS, SS, and LF)

d. Bounding Theory
The Subjacency Condition (at SS and/or LF)

e. Case Theory
The Case Filter (at SS)

f. Government Theory
The Empty Category Principle (ECP) (at SS and LF)

g. Binding Theory
Binding Principles (at SS and/or LF)

In science, the notion of **idea** is distinct from that of **execution**. It's one thing to **explain** that there's light in nature; it's an entirely different matter to **prove** the existence of light. For instance, the existence of light can be explained by Particle Theory or Wave Theory.

The **X'-schema** is a core part of the **Phrase Structure Theory** called **X'-theory**. Since Chomsky (1994), X'-theory has been replaced with the **Bare Phrase Structure Theory**. The **PRO Theorem** is a core part of **Control Theory**. The **θ-criterion** and the **Projection Principle** are central parts of **θ-theory**. The **Subjacency Condition** is an instantiation of **Bounding Theory**. The **Case Filter** is an integral part of **Case Theory**. In GB, Case licensing is formulated as **Case assignment**. In Minimalism, it is reformulated as **Case checking**. The **ECP** is a central part of **Government Theory**. **Binding Theory** has the shape of three Binding **Conditions** (i.e., Principle A, Principle B, and Principle C). Later on, Chomsky and Lasnik (1995) explore an **interpretive** version of Binding Theory.

There have been various efforts of unifying two or more modules into one. For instance, Chomsky (1986b) attempts to unify **Government** Theory and **Bounding** Theory via the notion of ***barriers***.

Exercise 1

《1-1》

Explain the architecture of Chomsky's (*LGB*) Universal Grammar. (Do not exceed the length of 5 lines.)

《1-2》

Discuss the fundamental properties of a sentence. (Do not exceed the length of 5 lines.)

《1-3》

How many levels of representation are there in the P&P model? Define each level. (Do not exceed the length of 10 lines.)

《1-4》

Explain what covert movement operations are, illustrating examples. (Do not exceed the length of 10 lines.)

《1-5》

Why is Government Theory a fundamental module in the P&P model? (Do not exceed the length of 10 lines.)

《1-6》

How many modues are there in the P&P model? Define each module very briefly. (Do not exceed the length of 20 lines.)

2 X-bar Theory

Every phrase has the similar **hierarchical** (**three-level**) structure. Each type of phrase is generated by similar Phrase Structure (**PS**) rules. Thus, we don't need particular rules to generate each type of phrase. **X-bar** (**X'**) Theory is **innate** (part of UG). It provides the child with the general format of PS rules, greatly simplifying the task of **acquisition**. Lexical and functional phrases have the same X'-structure.

2.1 VP, PP, NP, and AP

The PS component contains PS rules such as the following:

(1)	a.	S	→	NP (Aux) VP
	b.	VP	→	V (NP) ({NP, PP}) (S)
	c.	NP	→	(Det) N (PP) (S)

One motivation for **X'-theory** is to eliminate a **redundancy** in Chomsky's (1965) *Aspects* model. That is, the information about possible phrase structures is coded twice, both in **PS rules** such as (1b) and in **lexical entries** such as (2).

(2) a. run: +v, [___]
b. love: +v, [___ NP]
c. claim: +v, [___ S]
d. give: +v, [___ NP {NP, PP}]
e. tell: +v, [___ NP S]

Given (1), for instance, (3) can be generated.

(3)

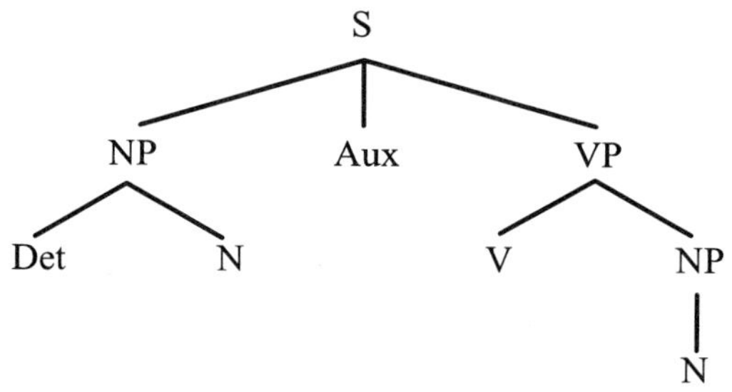

By way of a process of lexical insertion, (4) can be derived.

(4)

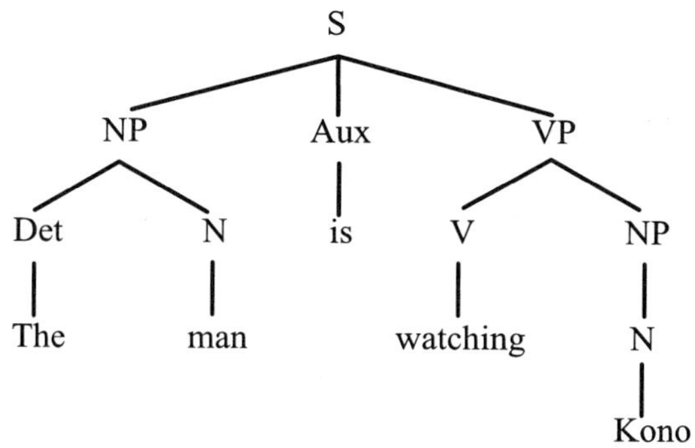

Endocentricity means headness. For instance, an NP must have an N.

(5) a. NP → N
b. *NP → A PP

We need only to examine the head of a phrase. The following shows that there is a **thematic** relation between a V and its object:

(6) a. Steve ate bagels.
b. *Steve ate principles.
c. *Steve ate principles of bagel making.

(7) a. Steve ate [$_{NP}$ {Danny's, no, every} bagel].
b. I ate [$_{NP}$ a big fat greasy luscious chocolate square bagel with no hole].

In X'-theory, endocentricity is expressed as follows:

(8) XP → ... X ...

The following shows an X'-theoretic tree structure:

(9)

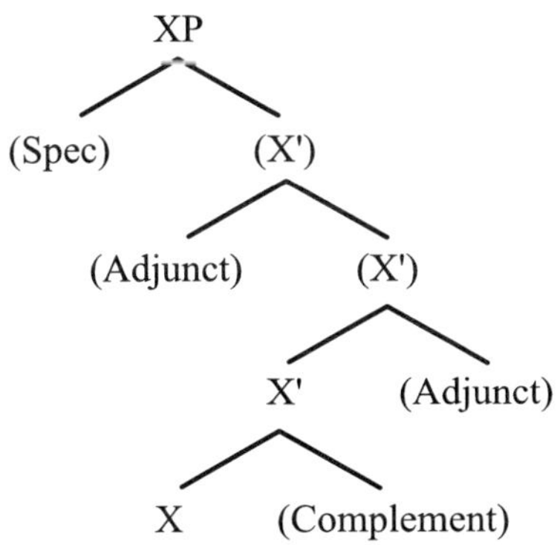

A **head** decides the status of **dependents**. A **complement** is always a sister of the head. A **specifier** is an immediate constituent of a maximal phrasal projection of the head. An **adjunct** is a constituent which adjoins to an intermediate (i.e., X') projection, creating an adjunction structure.♣ Adjuncts are introduced by a recursive rule.

♣ At the moment, we simply assume that an adjunct adjoins to an X'-projection as in (9). However, it has been reported that X'-projections are invisible for grammatical operations. Given this, we will assume later that an adjunct is adjoined only to Xs or XPs. See section 2.6.

(10) a. X' → X' YP

b. X' → YP X'

Complements are semantically distinct from adjuncts in that the former is selected by a head whereas the latter is not.

(11) Steve fixed *(the car) (yesterday).

COMPLEMENT ADJUNCT

For instance, let's consider the X'-theoretic structure of nominals. The following shows a multiple branching structure of NP:

(12)

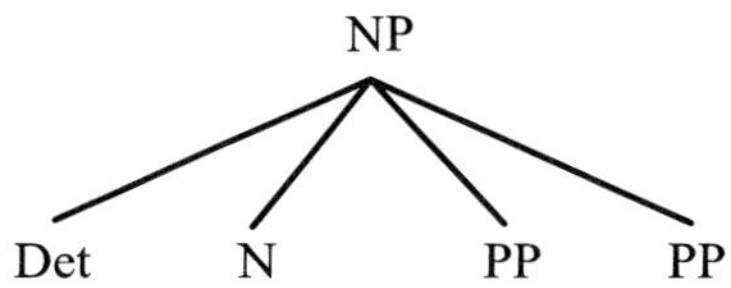

There is evidence that the **binary branching** structure in (13) is superior to the multiple branching structure in (12).

(13)

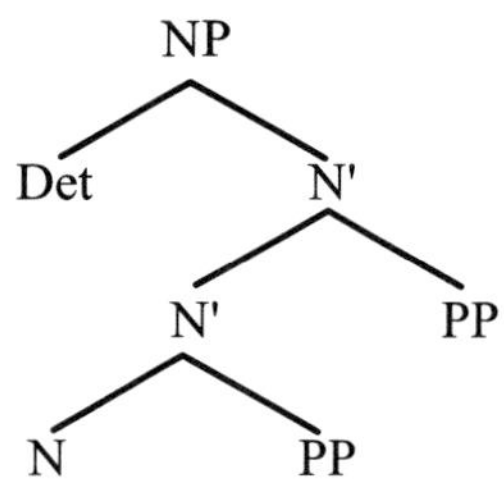

EVIDENCE

***One* pronominalization** shows that the pronominal *one* can replace either the head noun plus a complement PP as in (14a) or the head noun, a complement PP, and an adjunct PP as in (14b).

(14) a. Steve met this [student] [of physics] with long hair, and Danny met that one with short hair.

b. Steve met this [student] [of physics] [with long hair], and Danny met that one.

As shown below, the binary branching structure captures the above replacement possibilities, but the multiple branching structure does not because the replacement targets do not form a constituent in the latter.

(15) a.

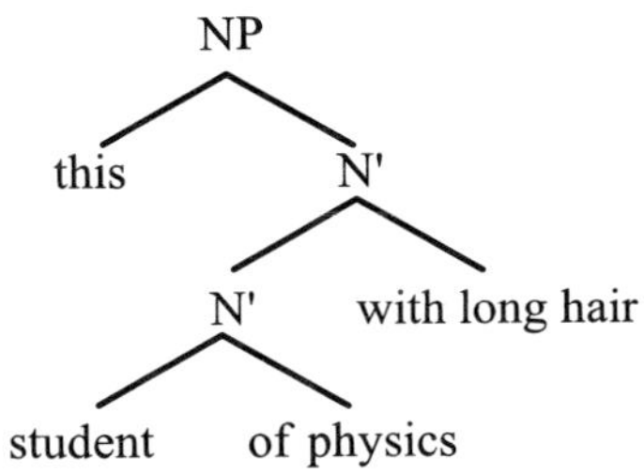

b.

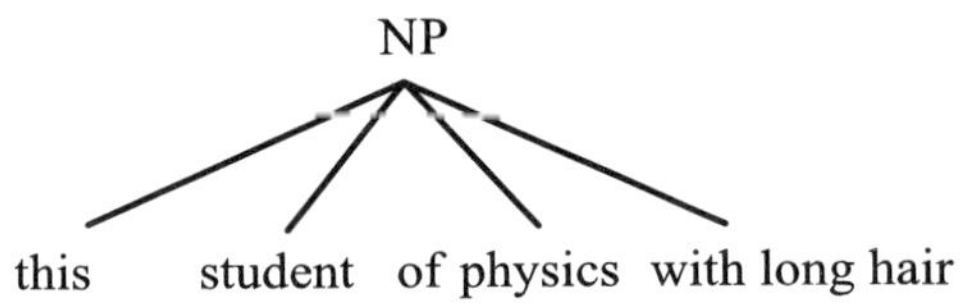

The X'-theoretic tree of (16) is (17).

(16) this prince

(17)

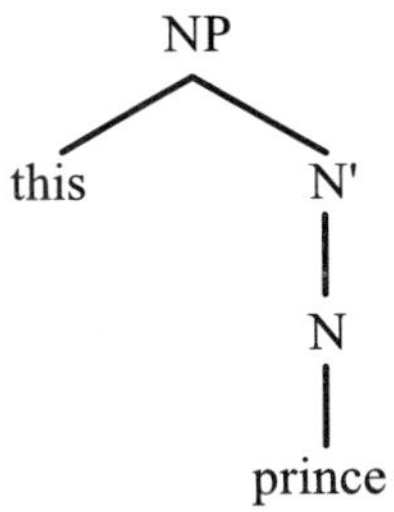

The X'-theoretic tree of (18) is (19).

(18) this prince of Denmark with a nasty temper

(19)

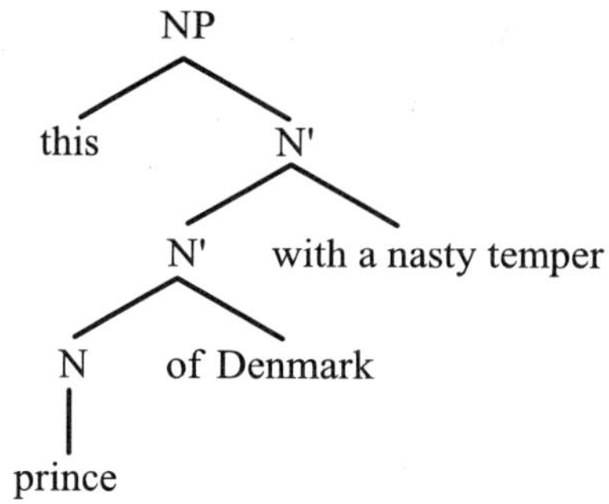

The proform *one* targets X'-projection:

(20) a. Steve likes this [$_{N'/N}$ prince], and I like that one.
b. *Steve likes this [$_{N}$ prince] of Denmark, and I like that one of France.

(21a) says two properties about Hamlet. (21b) says just one property about him.

(21) a. Hamlet is a prince from Denmark.
'He is a prince (possibly of some other country), and he is from Denmark.'
b. Hamlet is a prince of Denmark.
'He is a Denmark prince.'

According to X'-theory, a complement should be adjacent to its head. Thus, the complement must precede the adjunct in (22). However, there is no fixed word order between adjuncts as in (23).

(22) a. the prince of Denmark with a nasty temper
b. *the prince with a nasty temper of Denmark

(23) a. the prince from Denmark with a nasty temper
b. the prince with a nasty temper from Denmark

Adjuncts can iterate, but determiners cannot:

(24) a. the prince from Denmark with a nasty temper
b. *this the prince from Denmark

2.2 IP and CP

V, P, N, and A/Adv are **lexical categories**. They are also called **major categories** in that they express the basic content of the proposition as *thematic* categories.

I, C, and D are **functional categories**. They are also called **minor categories**. They play no active role with respect to licensing θ-roles.

In the following, the modal Aux *must* adds the extra overtone that *her disappearance* is an obligation. The complementizer *that* introduces a declarative embedded clause.

(25) Steve said that_C she must_I disappear.

The complementizer *if* introduces an interrogative embedded clause.

(26) Steve asked if_C she must disappear.

Endocentricity is not an intrinsic property of every PS system. This is one motivation for the introduction of X'-theory. Two rules, which are not compatible with X'-theory, make their way into GB (Chomsky *LGB*):

(27) a. S' → COMP S
b. S → NP Aux VP

The following is outside of X'-theory. What is the head of S?

(28)

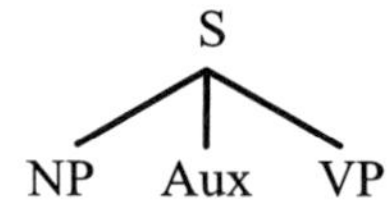

Modal Auxes, the nonfinite marker *to*, and the finite inflection -*s* carry inflections.

(29) a. Steve will leave.
b. I expect [Steve to leave].
c. Steve always leaves.

For instance, *will* and -*s* show complementary distribution.

(30) *Steve will leaves.

(28) is revised as (31) where Inflection = INFL = I. (31) is further revised as (32). We assume that INFL is the head of S = IP.

(31)

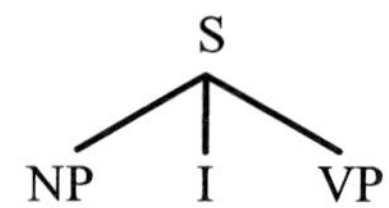

(32) a. IP → NP I'
b. I' → I VP

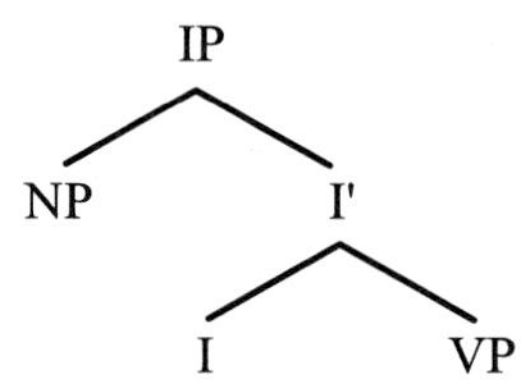

The following I' coordination suggests that I and VP form a single constituent, marked as I'.

(33) He $[_{I'}$ may $[_{VP}$ attend the conference]] but $[_{I'}$ won't $[_{VP}$ present a paper]].

In some cases, a head and its specifier have an agreement relation as in (34).

(34) a. $[_{NP}$ {this, *these} $[_{N'}$ book]]

b. $[_{NP}$ {*this, these} $[_{N'}$ books]]

The Specifier-Head agreement relation in (34) generalizes to the subject NP of a finite clause since a subject must agree in number and person with the inflected form of a V or Aux. A subject is thus regarded as the specifier of IP.

(35) a. Steve loves Kono.

b. $[_{IP}$ Steve $[_{I'}$ [pres] $[_{VP}$ love Kono]]]

Every element conforms to X'-theory. The complementizer *that* selects a finite embedded clause, and the complementizer *for* a nonfinite embedded clause. That is, there is a selectional restriction between the embedded C and the embedded I, dubbed as a Head-to-Head relation.

(36) a. I think $that_C$ $[_{IP}$ he knows the answer]. [+FINITE]

b. I was anxious for_C $[_{IP}$ him to know the answer]. [-FINITE]

In this light, the revision of (27a) is as follows:

(37)	a.	CP	→	(Spec)	C'
	b.	C'	→	C	IP

(38) is revised as (39).

(38)

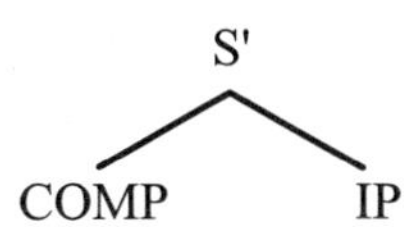

(39)

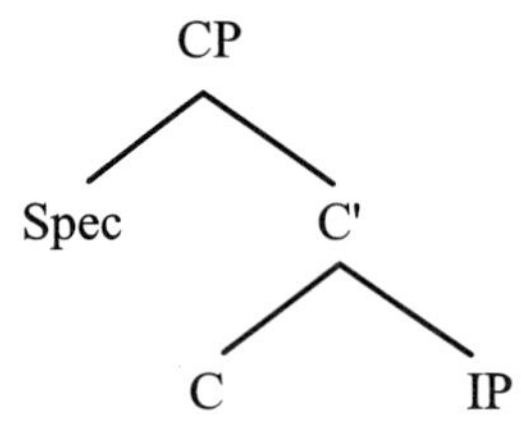

The specifier position in CP depends on the Specifier-Head agreement relation, as illustrated in (40) for the sentential complements of the V *wonder*.

(40) a. I wonder$_V$ [$_{CP}$ ∅ {whether, if}$_C$ the economy will recover in the future].

b. *I wonder$_V$ [$_{CP}$ ∅ that$_C$ the economy will recover in the future].

c. I wonder$_V$ [$_{CP}$ in which year [+wh]$_C$ the economy will recover].

There is a **selectional restriction** between a matrix V and its embedded C. For instance, (40) follows from a selectional restriction (a Head-to-Head relation) that a matrix V imposes on the head of its CP complement. (40b) violates the selectional restriction, whereas (40a), assuming that *whether* and *if* are instances of C, satisfies it; *wonder* selects an interrogative C. (40c) does not directly satisfy this restriction because the PP *in which year* cannot be taken as an instance of C. However, (40c) satisfies the selectional restriction indirectly, given the Specifier-Head agreement between the [+wh] C and the PP in Spec of CP.

To summarize, CP introduces the **force** of a sentence. IP introduces the **finiteness** of a sentence. VP introduces the **basic proposition** expressed by a sentence.

If S' = CP and S = IP, every phrase conforms to X'-theory.

(41)

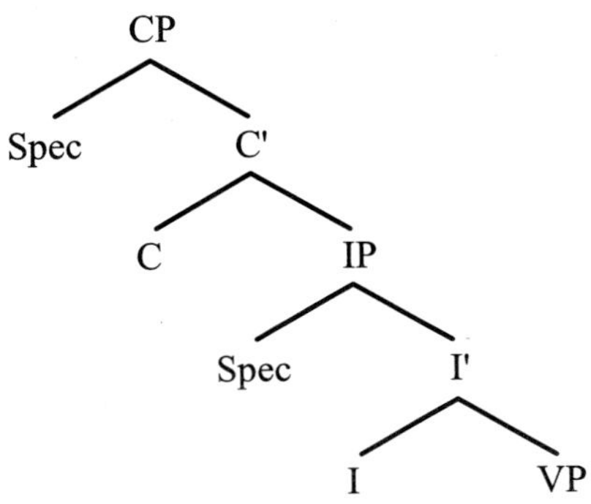

2.3 DP

In English, determiners (e.g., *a, the*) and possessors (e.g., *John's, his*) are mutually exclusive.

(42)

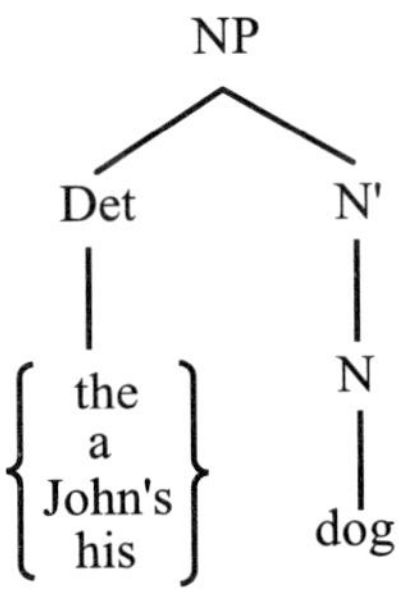

In Hungarian, determiners and possessors can co-occur in a nominal string.

(43) a Józsi kutyája
the Józsi dog-3sg
'Józsi's dog'

Let's assume that a determiner D is the head of a nominal phrase. It decides the property of **(in)definiteness** of the nominal phrase. For instance, in (44a) *the* is the head of DP, and *dog* is the head of NP.

(44) a. [$_{DP}$ the [$_{NP}$ dog in the room]]

b. [$_{DP}$ a [$_{NP}$ dog in the room]]

Abney (1987) proposes a **DP hypothesis** that a determiner head projects a DP. The following structure is in compliance with X'-theory.

(45)

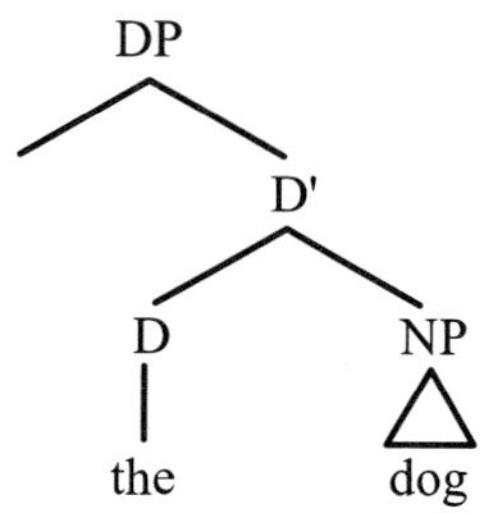

Abney proposes that an abstract D (*pos*) obligatorily accompanies a possessor and that this phonologically null morpheme is mutually exclusive with other Ds.

(46) a. his *pos* dog

b. the dog

c. *his *pos* the dog

(47a) is Abney's DP structure of (46a). (47b) is a variant of (47a). (47c) and (47d) are the correspondents of (47a) and (47b), respectively, if *his* or *he* was underlyingly inserted into Spec of NP. Note that it is beyond syntax how to amalgamate *he* and *'s* at a later derivation in (47b) and (47d).

(47) a.

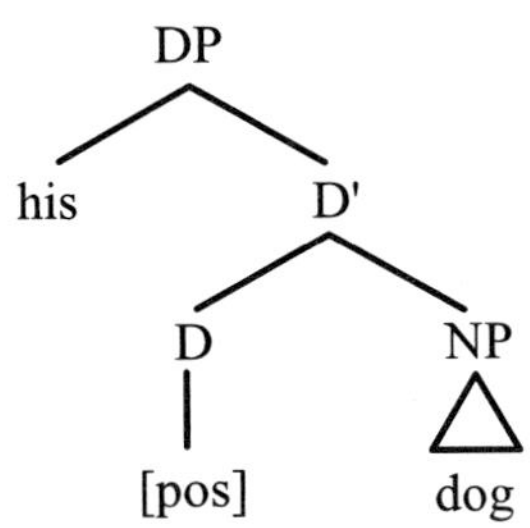

b.

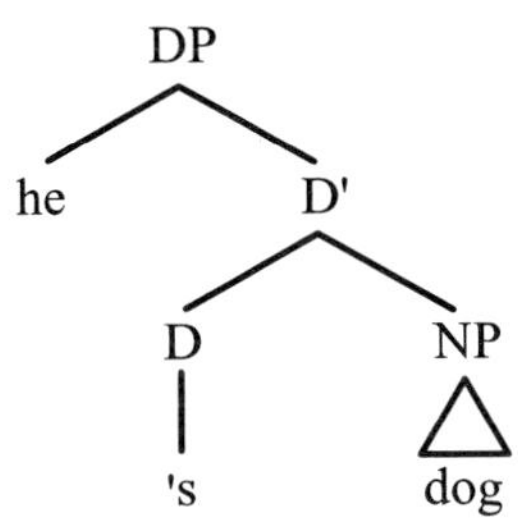

c.

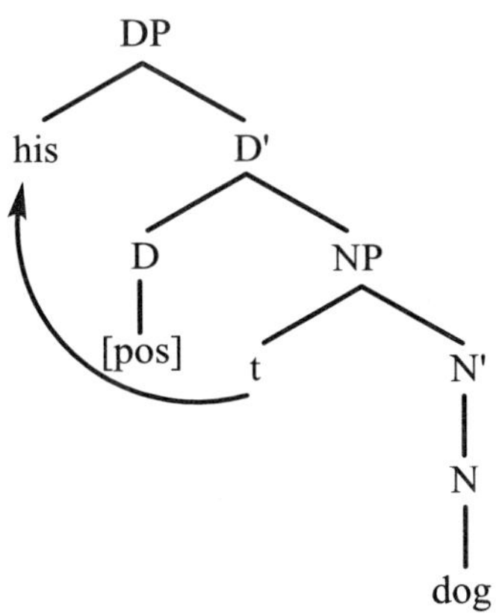

d.

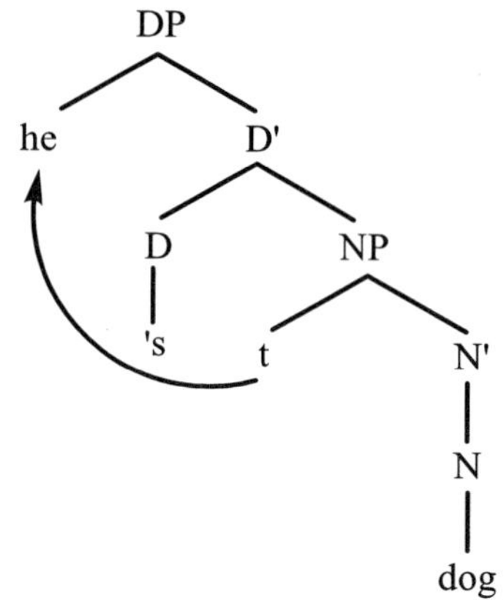

Proper Ns usually have no Ds because they are **inherently definite**, but may occur with them under certain circumstances.

(48) a. *The Kono left.
b. She's not the Kono that I used to know.
c. There's a Kono at the door.

Pronouns cannot occur with Ds under any circumstance.

(49) a. *The she left.
b. *She's not the her that I used to know.
c. *There's a her at the door.

Let's assume that pronouns replace not N but D.

(50)

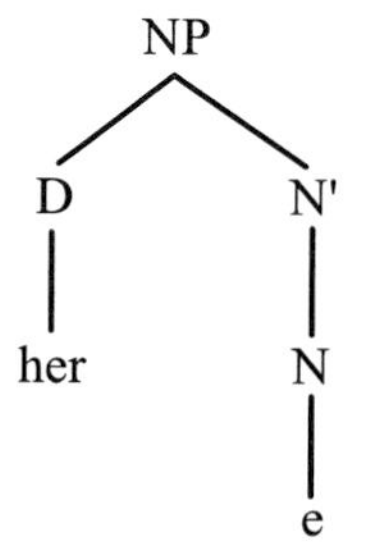

Under a DP hypothesis, pronouns are regarded as intransitive Ds.

(51)

Determiners are used **prenominally** as in (52a) or **pronominally** as in (52b).

(52) a. [$_{DP}$ We [$_{DP}$ Yanks]] do envy you Brits.

b. [$_{DP}$ We] do envy you.

The following is a two-year old child's utterance. In (53) *it* was used as a prenominal D.

(53) Get it ladder!

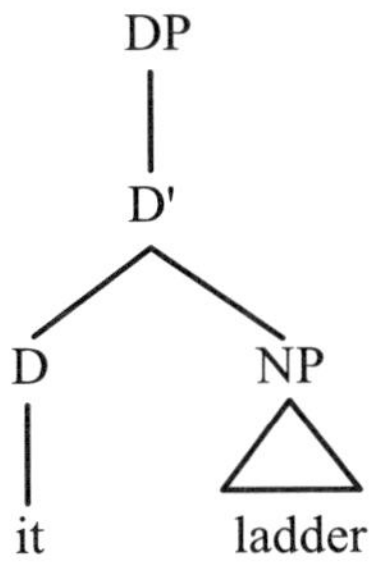

A DP may have more structure. The following DP involves internal movements. In (55) *ing* is analyzed as a nominalizer, selecting VP as its complement. Gerund phrases are internally VPs (taking a nominal complement) and externally DPs (playing the role of an argument).

(54) *Steve's writing poems* impressed his students.

(55)

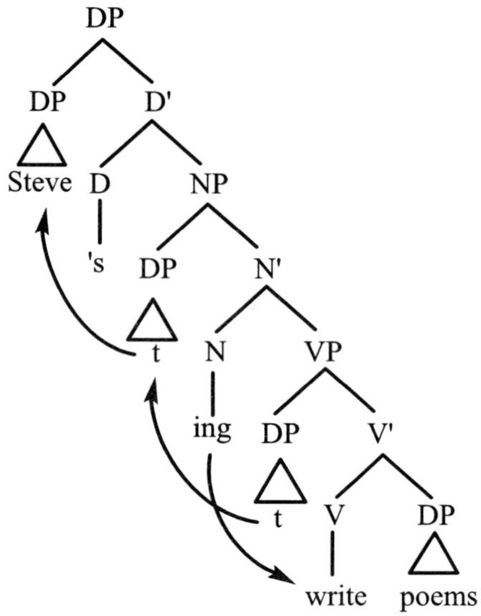

To summarize, the DP hypothesis makes two important claims.

(56) a. The structure of nominals fully conforms to X'- theory.
b. The structural relation between D and NP is a Head-Complement relation.

There is evidence of the **null determiner** ∅: generic sense, partitive sense, and quantificational sense.

(57) a. The Italians do love the opera.
b. Italians do love opera.

(58) a. $[_{DP}$ The $[_{NP}$ Italians]] do love $[_{DP}$ the $[_{NP}$ opera]].
b. $[_{DP}$ ∅ $[_{NP}$ Italians]] do love $[_{DP}$ ∅ $[_{NP}$ opera]].

The shaded Ns below have the **generic** interpretation.

(59) a. Eggs are fattening.
b. Bacon is fattening.

The shaded Ns below have the **partitive** interpretation.

(60) a. I had eggs for breakfast.
b. I had bacon for breakfast.

Null determiners have the **quantificational** properties.

(61) a. We don't have enough {machinery, machines, *machine}.
b. Never trust ∅ {machinery, machines, *machine}.

There is mirror image between nominals and clauses. Given the Predicate-Internal Subject Hypothesis (PISH), the IP structure of clauses parallels the DP structure of nominals.♣

(62) a. his jump over the fence

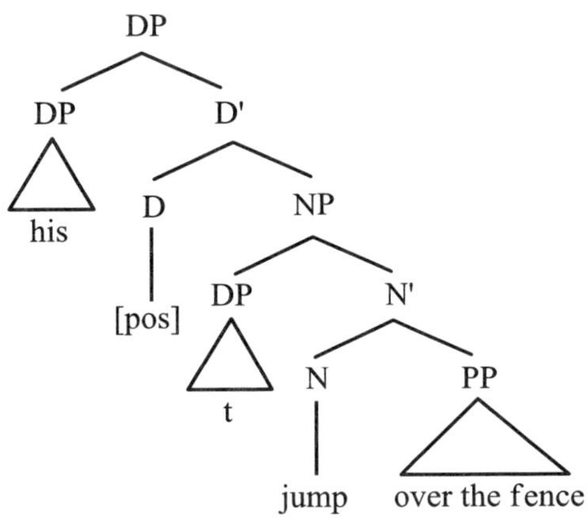

♣ See section 3.4 for the motivation of the PISH.

b. He jumped over the fence.

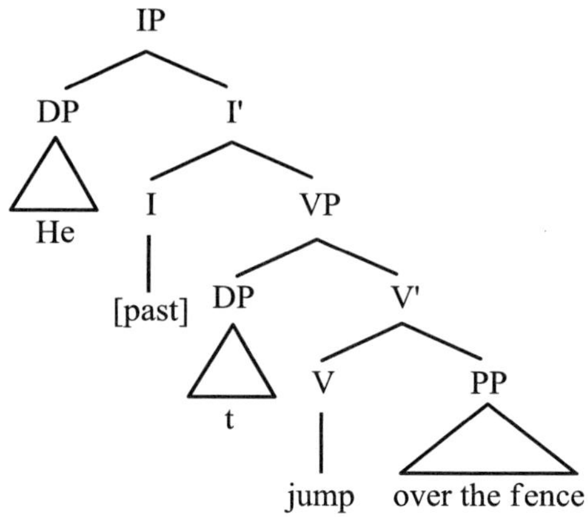

It has been reported that post-Ds such as *many, few*, or *several* may occur with Ds as in (63a) but are not recursive as in (63b), contra recursive adjectives as in (63c) and (63d). They should precede adjectives as in (63e).

(63) a. those many stupid ideas
b. *those many several stupid ideas
c. those many stupid ambitious ideas
d. those many ambitious stupid ideas
e. *those stupid many ideas

According to Abney (1987), post-Ds occupy Spec of NP.

(64)

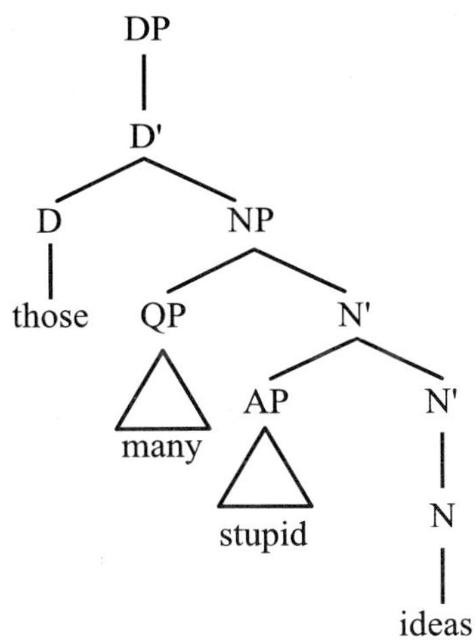

2.4 VP Shell

The V *receive* is ditransitive, thus requiring two complements. If the **Sisterhood Condition** holds between a head and its complements, the X'-theoretic tree assumed so far predicts that the VP headed by *receive* allows ternary branching.

(65)

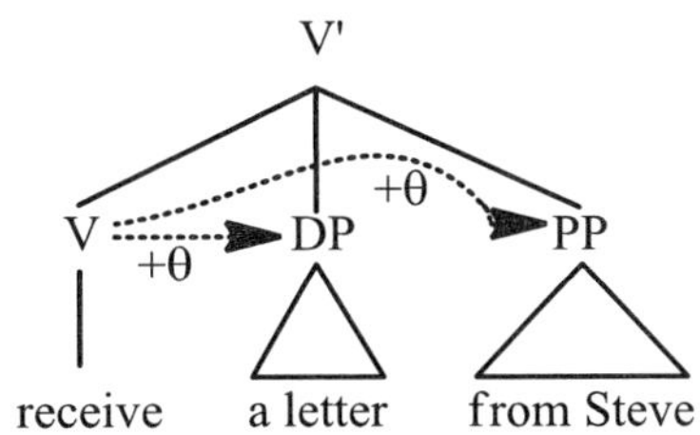

Suppose that the **Binary Branching Condition** is fundamental. If we keep the condition, we had better give up the previous definitions of complements (sisters of an X) and adjuncts (sisters of an X' and daughters of an X'). Let's define complements and adjuncts in terms of their **semantic** relations to the head X.

(66) a. **Complements** are selected by the head and therefore appear in the head's subcategorization frame.

b. **Adjuncts** are non-selected modifiers and do not appear in the subcategorization frame.

The **Sisterhood Condition on θ-role assignment** guarantees that complements are structurally closer and more string-adjacent to the head than adjuncts are. One proviso is to assume that undischarged θ-roles will be passed on to the immediately higher projection to be assigned to its sister as in (67). This assumption does not add any extra grammatical mechanisms because we already assume the indirect θ-licensing for the external θ-role as in (68).

(67)

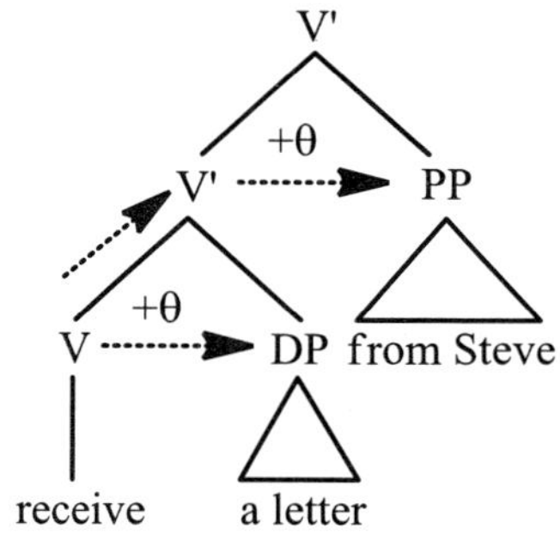

(68)

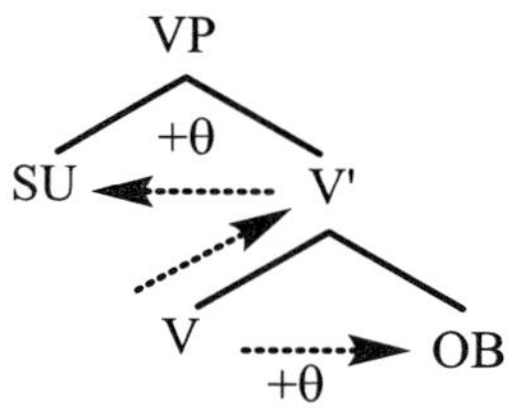

One potential problem of (67) is that the second complement is higher than the first one. Larson (1988) shows that the first complement is structurally higher than the second one.

Note that a reflexive object can refer to a subject, but not vice versa.

(69) a. Steve$_1$ congratulated himself$_1$.
b. *Himself$_1$ congratulated Steve$_1$.

There is evidence that the first complement c-commands the second complement.

A piece of evidence comes from **reflexive binding**.

EVIDENCE 1

(70) a. Steve showed Danny$_1$ himself$_1$ (in the mirror).
b. *Steve showed himself$_1$ Danny$_1$ (in the mirror).

Another piece of evidence comes from **NPI licensing**.

EVIDENCE 2

(71) a. No one likes anyone.
b. *Anyone likes no one.

(72) a. I told no one anything.
b. *I told anyone nothing.

Given this, the structure of (67) is revised as follows:

(73)

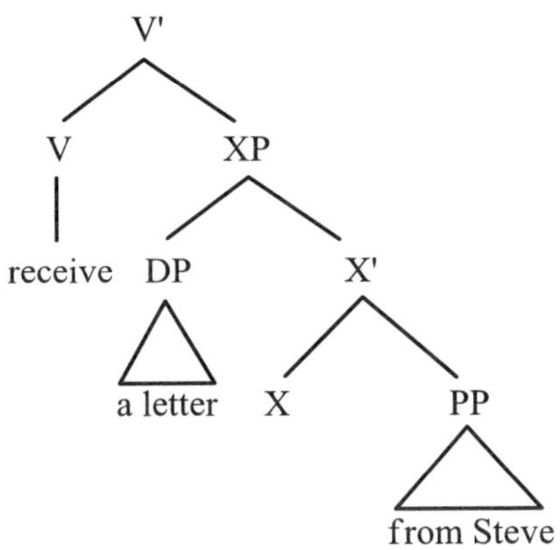

Let's assume that X = V. According to Larson's (1988) **VP Shell** hypothesis, ditransitive Vs assign θ-roles **derivationally**.♣

(74)

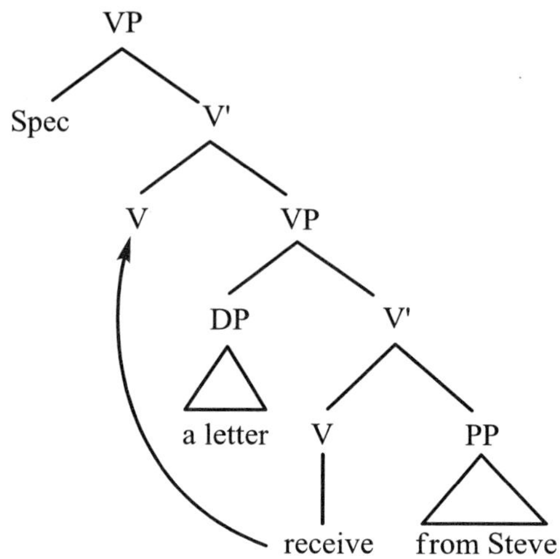

2.5 Coordination

Two or more elements can be connected with conjunctions such as *and*, *or*, and *but*.

CONJUNCTIVE (75) a. Steve and Kono went to the party.
DISJUNCTIVE b. Steve will go to the party or to the movies.
ADVERSATIVE c. Steve went to the party, but Kono remained home.

XPs can be coordinated.

(76) a. $[_{DP}$ the man] and $[_{DP}$ a child]
b. $[_{VP}$ go to the library] and $[_{VP}$ read a book]
c. $[_{PP}$ down the stairs] and $[_{PP}$ out the door]

♣ See section 3.5 for further discussion of VP shell.

X-zeros or X-bars can also be coordinated.

(77) a. [$_P$ up] and [$_P$ down] the stairs

b. [$_V$ repair] and [$_V$ paint] the deck

(78) [never [$_{V'}$ drink alcohol] and [$_{V'}$ drive a car]]

In general, different categories cannot be coordinated.♣

(79) a. *He read [$_{DP}$ the book] and [$_{PP}$ in the library].

b. *He left [$_{DP}$ the house] and [$_{AP}$ very angry].

To summarize, coordination has the following schema. (80b) conforms to binary X'-theory.

(80) a.

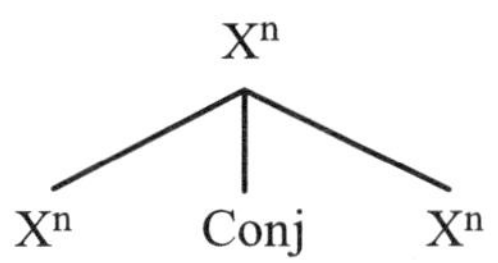

b.

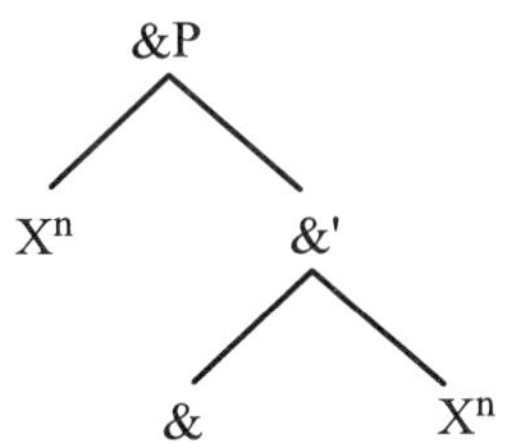

For instance, the following shows the structure of *write two books and ten papers*.

♣ In modern English, however, co-ordination with different categories is getting popular. Below, the shaded heads coordinate two complements.
(i) The reporter talks with an aviation expert about [$_{DP}$ turbulence] and [$_{CP}$ how pilots prepare for it].
(ii) An MIT Professor explains [$_{DP}$ the liquid metal battery] and [$_{CP}$ how it could change the way (that) we store and use energy].

(81) a.

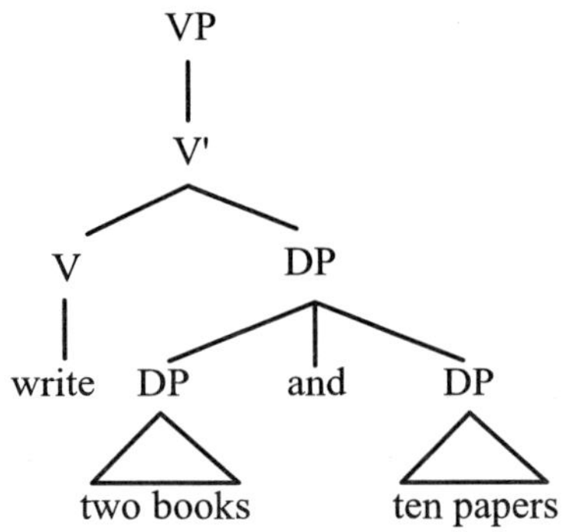

b.

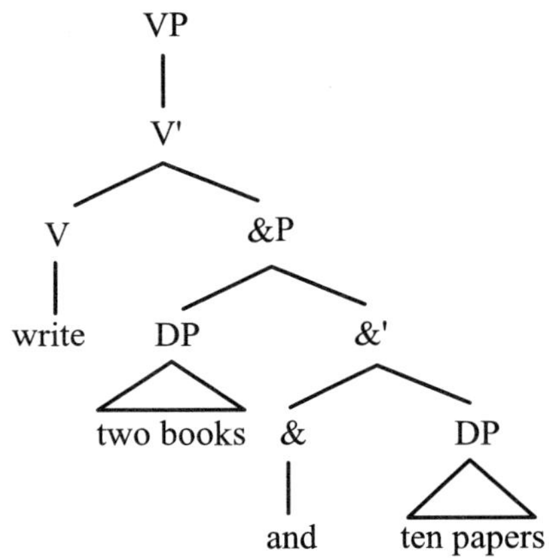

2.6 Eliminating X'

In Chomsky (*LGB*), determiners occupy Spec of NP:

(82) $[_{NP}$ D $[_{N'}$ N]]

However, DP is independently motivated:

(83) $[_{DP}$ D NP]

Do we need an N'-projection? The answer **was** yes.

One pronominalization has been a piece of evidence of an N'-projection:

(84) a. Steve likes this [$_{N'}$ prince] from Denmark, and I like that one from France.

b. *Steve likes this [$_{N}$ prince] of Denmark, and I like that one of France.

With the advent of DP, however, this evidence was undermined:

(85) a. Steve's discussion of the paper

b. [$_{DP}$ Steve$_1$ [$_{D'}$'s [$_{NP}$ t$_1$ [$_{N'}$ discussion of the paper]]]]

Let's give up the assumption that modifiers are adjuncts to X'. Instead, we suggest the following:

(86) Arguments are **dominated** by XP, and adjuncts are **adjoined** to XP.

Given this, *one* is a pro-NP, not a pro-N':

(87) a. [$_{DP}$ this [$_{NP}$ prince of Denmark]]

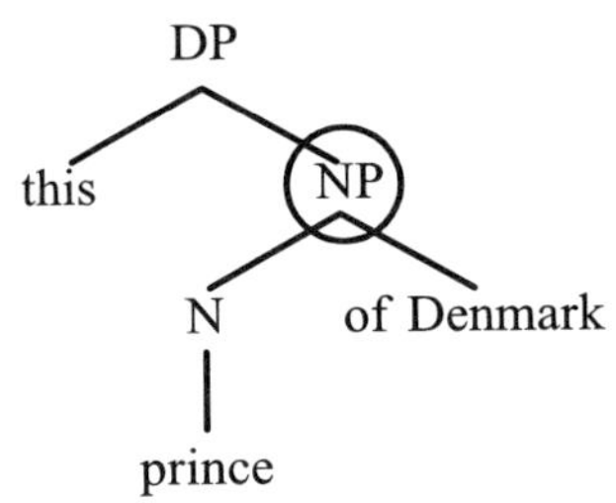

b. $[_{DP}$ this $[_{NP}$ $[_{NP}$ prince] [from Denmark]]]

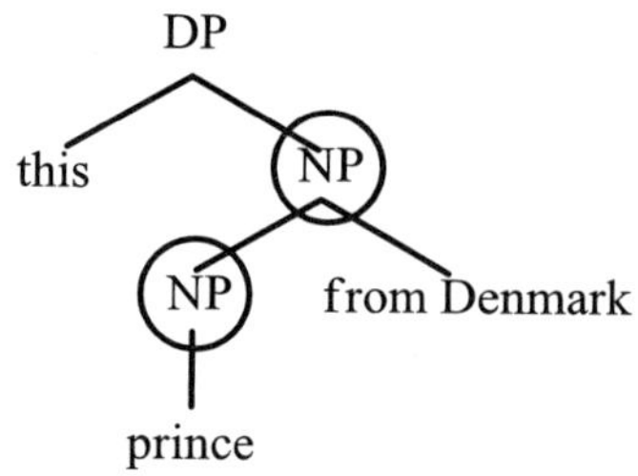

To summarize, the postulation of N' is not necessary. In this light, Minimalism gives up X'-theory, assuming that X' is invisible for an operation or useless for building up phrase structure.

Exercise 2

《2-1》

Discuss the redundancy in Chomsky's *Aspects* model, illustrating examples. (Do not exceed the length of 10 lines.)

《2-2》

Discuss the selectional restriction between the embedded C and the embedded I, illustrating examples. (Do not exceed the length of 10 lines.)

《2-3》

Discuss the selectional restriction between the matrix V and the embedded C, illustrating examples. (Do not exceed the length of 10 lines.)

《2-4》

What do CP, IP, and VP introduce for building a sentence? (Do not exceed the length of 5 lines.)

《2-5》

Discuss the advantages of DP structure over NP structure, illustrating examples. (Do not exceed the length of 20 lines.)

《2-6》

What is the motivation for postulating null determiners? (Do not exceed the length of 20 lines.)

《2-7》

Discuss the parallel of IP strucure and DP structure, illustrating relevant examples. Assume the PISH, and draw trees. (Do not exceed the length of 20 lines.)

《2-8》

How can we treat post-determiners given X'-theory? Explore at least one possibility. (Do not exceed the length of 20 lines.)

《2-9》

Discuss how to analyze the structure of a ditransitve verb, given the Binary Branching Condition. (Do not exceed the length of 20 lines.)

《2-10》

Define the notions of a complement and an adjunct, given the Binary Branching Condition. (Do not exceed the length of 10 lines.)

《2-11》

Discuss the evidence that the first complement of a ditransitive verb is higher than the second complement. (Do not exceed the length of 20 lines.)

3 θ-theory

θ-theory is concerned with the thematic relations between θ-assigners (i.e., lexical categories such as V, P, N, or A) and θ-assignees (e.g., argument DPs, CPs, or PPs). The core principle of θ-theory is the θ-criterion according to which there should be a one-to-one correspondence between θ-roles and arguments.

3.1 Trace

No movement can radically alter a structure. If an element moves, it leaves behind a trace in its original position.

There is evidence of traces.

The **contraction** involving topicalization and wh-movement suggests that a moved element leaves a trace. EVIDENCE 1

The following shows embedded **topicalization**.

(1) a. This problem, [$_{IP}$ Kono thinks [$_{IP}$ Steve solved ___]].

b. This student, [$_{IP}$ Kono thinks [$_{IP}$ ___ solved this problem]].

(2a) can be pronounced as (2b). This is called ***wanna* contraction**.

(2) a. You want to solve this problem.
b. You wanna solve this problem.

Wanna contraction requires **adjacency**.

(3) a. You want [$_{IP}$ this student to solve this problem].
b. *You wanna this student solve this problem.

Contraction is banned after the topicalization of a subject.

(4) a. This student, you want ___ to solve this problem.
b. *This student, you wanna solve this problem.

Contraction is still banned after wh-movement.

(5) a. Which student do you want ___ to solve this problem?
b. *Which student do you wanna solve this problem?

It is concluded that the intervening trace between *want* and *to* bans contraction.

The lost ambiguity in *wanna* contraction confirms the presence of a trace. (6) is ambiguous between (6A) reading and (6B) reading. However, (7) is not ambiguous. It has only one reading in (7A).

(6) Who did the coach want to shoot at the end of the game?
A. He wanted to shoot Kono at the end of the game.
B. He wanted Kono to shoot at the end of the game.

(7) Who did the coach wanna shoot at the end of the game?
A. He wanted to shoot Kono at the end of the game.

The contracted form *'ve* can be attached to a word which ends in a vowel or diphthong as in (8). However, the contraction in (9b) is not permitted.

(8) a. I have been to Hawaii.
b. I've been to Hawaii.

(9) a. Which students would you say have got most out of the course?
b. *Which students would you say've got most out of the course?

We propose that the presence of the intervening trace (i.e., wh-trace) prevents *have* from contracting into *say*.

(10) a. you would say which students have got most out of the course — DS
b. Which students$_1$ would you say t_1 have got most out of the course? — SS

Traces are not empty but silent when it comes to syntax.

The subject-verb **agreement** suggests that a moved element leaves a trace. — EVIDENCE 2

It has been observed that agreement is a **local** process.

(11) a. They think [$_{IP}$ he likes psychology].
b. *They think [$_{IP}$ he like psychology].

However, apparent **long-distance** agreement obtains. The following shows that a topicalized phrase or a wh-phrase **had** a local relation with an embedded V, respectively, at DS. This agreement relation is conveyed via traces at SS.

(12) a. This student$_1$, they think [$_{IP}$ t_1 {likes, *like} it].
b. Which student$_1$ do they think [$_{IP}$ t_1 {likes, *like} it]?

Head movement suggests that a moved element leaves a trace. — EVIDENCE 3

In English, an aspectual Aux like *have* can move from V to I, and only in I can the contracted negation *n't* attach to the Aux.

(13) He hasn't read the paper.

(14) a. he $[\text{pres}]_I$ **not** $[_{VP}$ **have** read the paper]
b. he **has$_I$ not** $[_{VP}$ ___$_V$ read the paper]
c. he **hasn't$_I$** $[_{VP}$ ___$_V$ read the paper]

In (15) the modal *will* moves to C, vacating the I position. The ungrammaticality of (15) indicates that the movement of *have* to I is impossible. The reason is that when an element moves, the position it vacates is not entirely empty but filled by a trace of the moved element.

(15) *Will$_C$ he haven't$_I$ ___ read the paper?

(16)

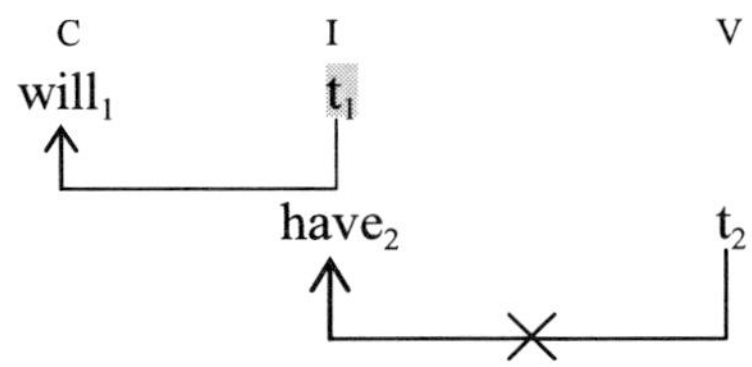

3.2 The Projection Principle

The **Projection Principle** states that lexical information is syntactically represented at all syntactic levels.

(17) The Projection Principle
Representations at each **syntactic level** (i.e., DS, SS, and LF) are projected from the Lexicon in that they observe the subcategorization properties of lexical items.

For instance, in (18b) the selectional properties of the verb *hit* are not correctly projected, thus violating the C-selection and S-selection properties of the V, the θ-criterion, and the Projection Principle.

(18) a. Steve hit the table.
b. *Steve hit.

The **Extended Projection Principle (EPP)** is the extended/extra part of the Projection Principle, asserting that all clauses must contain a subject.

(19) The Extended Projection Principle
All clauses must have an **overt** or **covert** subject.

The following sentences are ungrammatical due to the violation of the EPP.♣

(20) a. *Is illegal to park your car here.
b. *Is a man in the garden.

In order to satisfy the EPP, expletives such as *it* or *there* may be inserted in the subject position. They are semantically void and just place-holders of the subject position.

(21) a. It is illegal to park your car here.
b. There is a man in the garden.

3.3 The θ-criterion

A **predicate** expresses a state or an action, and an **argument** plays a role in that state or action.

θ-roles are **semantic** roles. Agent, Patient (or Theme), Goal (or Recipient), and Source are examples of θ-roles. Predicates assign θ-roles to their complements which occupy specific structural positions.

(22)	a.	Kamekona	drank	a pint of milk.	
		AGENT		PATIENT	
	b.	The government	banned	speeches fomenting terrorism.	
		AGENT		PATIENT	
	c.	Steve	sent	a letter	to Kono.
		SOURCE		PATIENT	RECIPIENT

♣
The covert subject such as PRO cannot appear in (20) in order to satisfy the EPP:
(i) a. *PRO is illegal to park your car here.
b. *PRO is a man in the garden.

PRO cannot be licensed in the subject position of a finite clause due to the PRO Theorem. See chapter 10.

d.	Kono RECIPIENT	received	a letter PATIENT	from Steve. SOURCE
e.	The dog AGENT	chewed	the slipper. PATIENT	
f.	The dog EXPERIENCER	saw	the slipper. THEME	

Lexical entries include C-selection (**subcategorization**) information and S-selection (**θ-grid**) information.

(23)	a.	chew:	[___ DP]	<AGENT, PATIENT>
	b.	receive:	[___ DP PP]	<RECIPIENT, THEME, SOURCE>
	c.	see:	[___ DP]	<EXPERIENCER, THEME>

The interpretation of an object is constant. That is, it is determined only by a verb. An object is an **internal argument**.

(24)	a.	Steve AGENT	broke	the window. PATIENT
	b.	The hammer INSTRUMENT	broke	the window. PATIENT

The interpretation of a subject is determined not solely by a verb but by a VP. A subject is an **external argument**.

(25)	a.	Steve AGENT INSTRUMENT	broke	the window.
	b.	Steve PATIENT AGENT INSTRUMENT	broke	his leg.

Let's assume that the ill-formed construction in (26a) is derived from the DS in (26b) via DP movement. ∅ indicates an empty DP.

(26) a. *It is easy [$_{CP}$ C [$_{IP}$ him$_1$ to like t$_1$]]. — SS — √CASE FILTER, *θ-CRITERION
-CASE +CASE
+θ +θ

b. (it) is easy [$_{CP}$ C [$_{IP}$ ∅ to like him]] — DS

Apparently, the **Case Filter** seems to play no role in (26a) because the chain of (*him, t*) formed via DP movement contains only one Case-marked position.♣

An empty DP, marked as *t*, is required for the derivations of both the simple passive construction as in (27a) and the raising construction as in (27b).

(27) a. Seymour$_1$ was [$_{VP}$ arrested t$_1$ in Shanghai]. — ∅ = t — √CASE FILTER, √θ-CRITERION
+CASE -CASE
-θ +θ

b. The situation$_1$ seems [$_{IP}$ t$_1$ to [$_{VP}$ be getting worse]]. — ∅ = t — √CASE FILTER, √θ-CRITERION
+CASE -CASE
-θ +θ

The subject and the object in active constructions receive independent θ-roles from an active verb. In passive constructions, however, the subject (i.e., external) θ-role is suppressed or assigned to the object of the preposition *by* if any. That is, the surface subject position in passives is nonthematic.

In raising constructions as in (27b), the nonthematic nature of the subject position is confirmed by the fact that pleonastic *it* may appear as in (28):

(28) It seems [$_{CP}$ that$_C$ [$_{IP}$ the situation is [$_{VP}$ getting worse]]].

Note that a thematic property easily differentiates the DP chain in (26a) from the one in (27a) and (27b). The DP in (26a) moves from a thematic position (object) to another thematic position (subject),

♣ See section 7.1. The Case Filter requires that every overt DP be assigned abstract Case.

whereas the DPs in (27a) and (27b) move from a thematic position to a nonthematic position. Given a theory of licensing θ-roles, the movement in (26a) can be prohibited by a constraint against arguments which receive more than one θ-role.

On the other hand, licensing θ-roles demands that every argument bear a θ-role. This request excludes the possibility of arguments in nonthematic positions. (29) illustrates this possibility.

*CASE FILTER
*θ-CRITERION

(29) a. *The student was praised the boy by the teacher.
+CASE -CASE +CASE
-θ +θ +θ

√CASE FILTER
*θ-CRITERION

b. *The situation seems that the economy is getting worse.
+CASE +CASE
-θ +θ

Although (29a) involves a Case Filter violation, (29b) does not. In this light, a constraint on licensing θ-roles is formulated being conjunctive as follows:

(30) The **θ-criterion** (Chomsky *LGB*: 36)
a. Each argument bears one and only one θ-role.
b. Each θ-role is assigned to one and only one argument.

The first part of the θ-criterion is stated in terms of θ-assignees, and the second part of the θ-criterion in terms of θ-assigners.

For instance, the Goal θ-role can be assigned in two different ways in ditransitive constructions. In (31) *Kono* bears the same semantic function with respect to the predicate *give*.

(31) a. Steve gave Kono a present.
GOAL

b. Steve gave a present to Kono.
GOAL

However, the Goal θ-role cannot be assigned to both an indirect object and a dative object simultaneously as in (32). This violates the **first** part of the θ-criterion as in (30a).

(32) *Steve gave Kono a present to Danny.
GOAL GOAL

*θ-CRITERION

Let's now consider (33). The predicate *mention* assigns two θ-roles. Since there is only one argument available for two θ-roles, (33) violates the **second** part of the θ-criterion as in (30b).

(33) *Danny mentioned ___ .
+θ ?θ

*θ-CRITERION

3.4 The Predicate-Interanl Subject Hypothesis (PISH)

In Chomsky (*LGB*), (35) is a SS structure of (34).

(34) Steve saw Kono.

(35) [$_{S}$ Steve Aux [$_{VP}$ see Kono]].♣

Given the **Binary Branching** Hypothesis and **Endocentricity**, (35) is revised as (36).

(36) [$_{IP}$ Steve [$_{I'}$ I [$_{VP}$ see Kono]]].

According to the Predicate-Interanl Subject Hypothesis (**PISH**), every θ-role of a head X is assigned within the projections of X.

(37) [$_{VP}$ Steve [$_{V'}$ see Kono]]

Due to the EPP, the VP-internal subject moves from Spec of VP to Spec of IP.

(38) [$_{IP}$ Steve$_1$ [$_{I'}$ I [$_{VP}$ t$_1$ [$_{V'}$ see Kono]]]].

There are some arguments for the PISH.

♣ Let's ignore the morphology of a main V.

ARGUMENT 1

Idioms must form a constituent as in (39a). What is interesting is that the sentential idiom in (39b) does not form a constituent at SS. Note that *the shit* is part of a larger sentential idiom, thus being non-referential, and that raising predicates do not impose selectional restrictions on their subjects.

(39) a. The shit hit the fan.
'Things got very bad.'
b. The shit seemed to hit the fan.

The following has an idiomatic reading, too. The idiomatic reading is **not affected** by the presence of modals, different tenses, different aspects, or negation.

(40) a. The shit {may, should, might, can} hit the fan.
b. The shit {hit, will hit, is hitting, has hit} the fan.
c. The shit did not hit the fan.

In fact, the idiom is just the VP indicated below; the other part becomes included as the derivation proceeds.

VP IDIOM

(41) [$_{VP}$ the shit [$_{V'}$ hit the fan]]

Tense, modals, negation, and aspect behave like raising predicates.

(42) [$_{IP}$ the shit$_1$ [$_{I'}$ {may, should, might, can} [$_{VP}$ t$_1$ [$_{V'}$ hit the fan]]]]

In short, the examples in (39) and (40) are regarded as sentential-level idioms in that they **were** a constituent within VP. This constitutes evidence for the PISH.

ARGUMENT 2

The CSC requests that nothing be extracted from a single conjunct although extraction is permissible from every conjunct in an ATB fashion.

(43) a. *[$_{CP}$ What$_1$ did [$_{IP}$ Steve eat t$_1$] and [$_{IP}$ Danny cook hamburgers]]?
b. [$_{CP}$ What$_1$ did [$_{IP}$ Steve eat t$_1$] and [$_{IP}$ Danny cook t$_1$]]?

Given this, consider the following:

(44) The girls will write a book and be awarded a prize for it.

PREDICATE-EXTERNAL SUBJECT HYPOTHESIS = PESH

If subjects originate in Spec of IP as in (45), (44) is predicted to be ungrammatical, due to violating the CSC.

(45) [$_{IP}$ the girls$_1$ will [$_{VP}$ write a book] and [$_{VP}$ be awarded t$_1$ a prize for it]]

PISH

However, if subjects originate in Spec of VP and are raised to Spec of IP as in (46), (44) is predicted to be grammatical. This reduces to an ATB extraction. Hence, the CSC fact in (44) provides evidence for the PISH.

(46) [$_{IP}$ the girls$_1$ will [$_{VP}$ t$_1$ write a book] and [$_{VP}$ be awarded t$_1$ a prize for it]]

ARGUMENT 3

The anaphor in (47a) is ambiguously interpreted, whereas that in (47b) is not. Note that the anaphor in the latter is contained within a fronted VP.

(47) a. Which stories about each other did they say [the kids liked t]? — AMBIGUOUS

b. ... but listen to each other, they say [the kids won't t]. — UNAMBIGUOUS

According to the PISH, the embedded clauses in (47) have the following underlying VPs, respectively.

(48) a. [$_{VP}$ the kids [$_{V'}$ liked [which stories about each other]]]

b. [$_{VP}$ the kids [$_{V'}$ listen to each other]]

During the derivational steps, the anaphor in (49a) was to be bound by both the embedded subject and the matrix subject. Given the PISH, however, the anaphor within a fronted VP as in (49b) has carried the **local binder**, the trace t$_2$, throughout the derivation. It is thus bound only by the embedded subject.

(49) a. $[_{CP}\ [_{DP}$ which stories about each other$]_1$ did $[_{IP}$ they say $[_{CP}\ t_1\ [_{IP}$ the kids$_2 [_{VP}\ t_2$ liked $t_1]]]]]$

b. $[_{CP}\ [_{VP}\ t_2$ listen to each other$]_1\ [_{IP}$ they say $[_{CP}\ t_1\ [_{IP}$ the kids$_2$ won't $t_1]]]]$

In short, the binding phenomenon within fronted VPs provides evidence for the PISH.

ARGUMENT 4

In the following, the (a) and (b) sentences are near-paraphrases of each other.

(50) a. All the men have left the party.

b. The men have all left the party.

(51) a. The women each seemed to eat a tomato.

b. The women seemed to each eat a tomato.

(52) a. Both the girls may sing arias in the production.

b. The girls may both sing arias in the production.

It can be proposed that quantifier floating results from the optionality of DP movement. The PISH captures the constituency between a quantifier and its host DP at DS. For instance, the following shows the derivation of (50b).

(53) $[_{IP}$ the men$_1\ [_{I'}$ have $[_{VP}\ [_{DP}$ all $t_1]$ left the party$]]]$

If the whole DP moves from Spec of VP to Spec of IP, (50a) is derived. In sum, quantifier floating supports the PISH.

ARGUMENT 5

Irish (Gaelic) is a V-initial language.♣

(54) Irish

Thóg	sí	teach	dófa	ar	an	Mhullach Dubh.
raised	she	house	for-them	on	the	Mullaghduff

'She built a house for them in Mullaghduff.'

♣ Gaelic is one of the Celtic languages, especially spoken in parts of Scotland and in Ireland.

How can we derive the VSO order? Given the PISH, let's assume that there is an **overt** V-to-I movement in Irish.

(55) $[_{IP}$ V_1+I $[_{VP}$ SU $[t_1$ OB]]]
V S O

African American Vernacular English (AAVE) permits the following word order. How is it possible, given the typical English word order of SVO?

(56) I know a way that can't nobody start a fight.

It can be assumed that AAVE does not have the EPP effect, thus allowing a VP-internal subject at SS.

(57) I know a way that can't $[_{VP}$ nobody start a fight].
I S V O

In short, certain word order facts provide evidence for the PISH.

3.5 Derivational θ-marking: VP Shell

The following has two internal arguments.

(58) Kono gave a book to Steve.
THEME GOAL

Below, the Theme is closer to the V than the Goal.

(59) [grammatical string but ill-formed treelet]

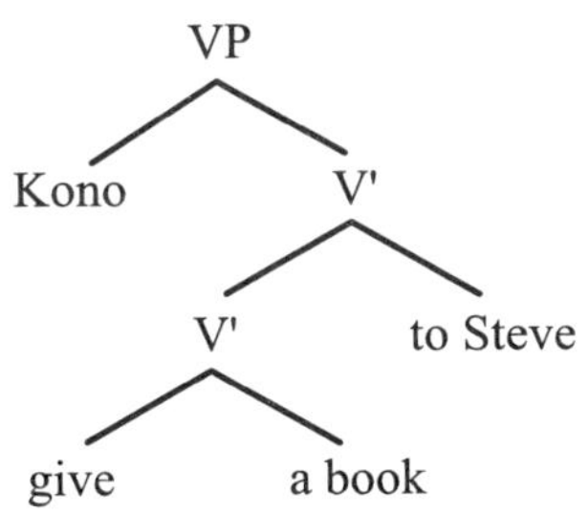

However, upon the careful examination of other data, (59) is not desirable.

In the following, *Kono* must c-command the anaphor in compliance with Principle A. That is, the first complement is structurally higher than the second complement.

(60) a. I presented/showed Kono to herself.
b. *I presented/showed herself to Kono.

Bound variable reading confirms this observation.

(61) a. I gave/sent every check$_1$ to its$_1$ owner.
b. ??I gave/sent his$_1$ paycheck to every worker$_1$.

NPI licensing shows that the first complement is higher than the second complement, too.

(62) a. I sent no presents to any of the children.
b. *I sent any of the packages to none of the children.

In addition, the Minimality Condition shows that the first complement is higher than the second complement.

(63) a. Which check did you send to whom?
b. *Whom did you send which check to?

For instance, let's consider the abstract representation of (60a) given below:

(64) [grammatical string but ill-formed treelet]

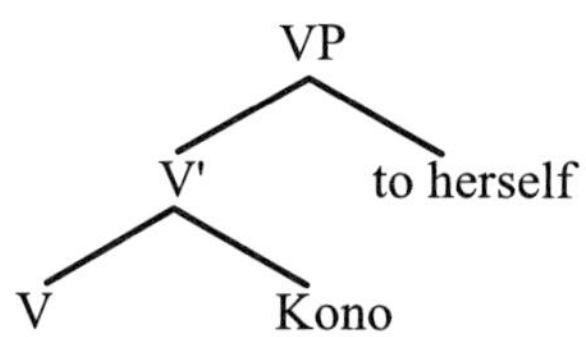

The abstract representation of (60b) is given below:

(65) [ungrammatical string and ill-formed treelet]

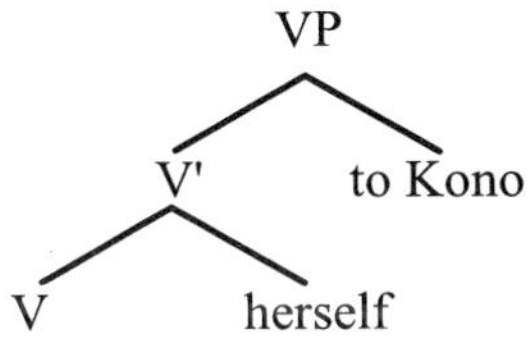

In short, the structure in (59) yields incorrect results.

If it is the Theme DP that c-commands the Goal PP within VP, we can account for the contrast in (60)-(63). As an illustration, consider again (60a) and (60b).

(66) [grammatical string and well-formed treelet]

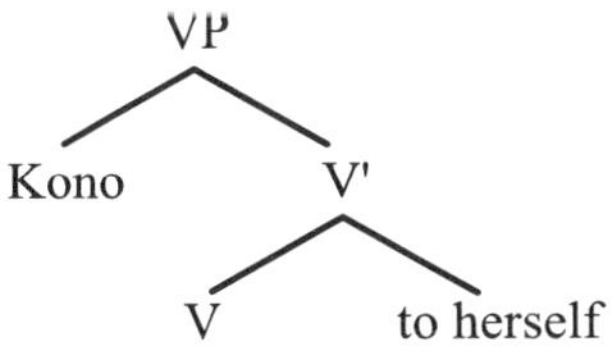

(67) [ungrammatical string and ill-formed treelet]

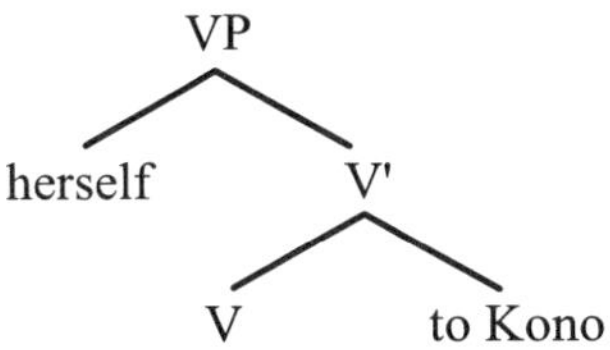

There is extra evidence against (59). Recall that idioms must form a constituent.

V'-IDIOMS

(68) a. Chin Ho *sent* his starting pitcher *to the showers*.♣
b. Kono *took* Steve *to the cleaners*.♣♣
c. Alex *threw* Danny *to the wolves*.♣♣♣
d. Kamekona *carries* such behavior *to extremes*.♣♣♣♣

As an illustration, a treelet (= partial structure) of (68a) is given in (69) where the Theme c-commands the Goal, and the V' corresponds to the idiomatic reading. That is, the following treelet provides the constituency which idioms demand.

(69)

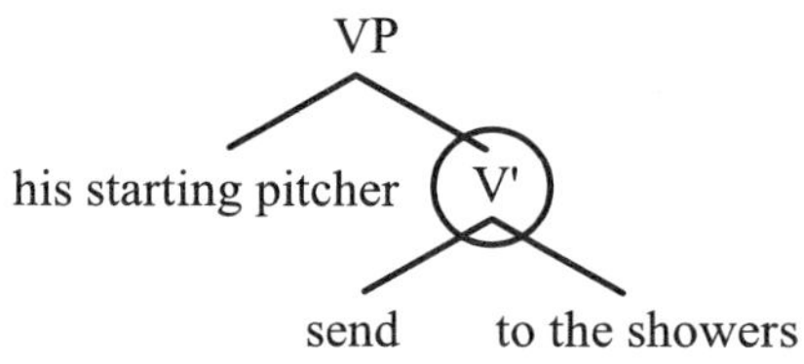

In short, the following is a more plausible structure of (58): cf. (59).

(70)

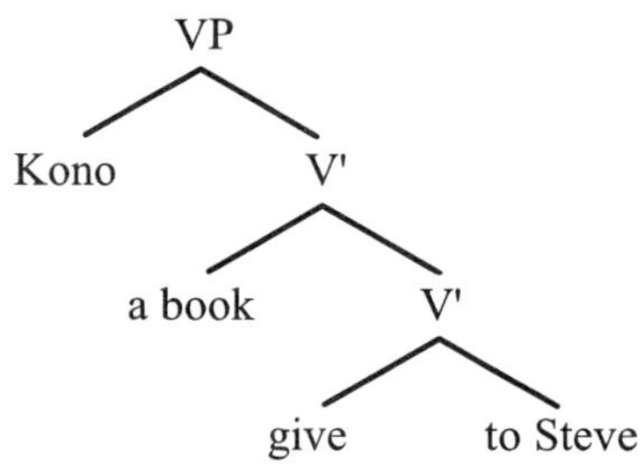

♣ *send sb to the showers*: 'to stop sb, especially sb on a sports team, from playing or working because they are behaving badly or their work is not good enough'

♣♣ *take sb to the cleaners*: 'to cheat sb and to take all their money or possessions or to defeat sb completely'

♣♣♣ *throw sb to the wolves*: 'to put sb in a situation in which they are severely criticized or attacked'

♣♣♣♣ *carry sth to extremes*: 'to do sth much more than is usual or reasonable'

In this light, Larson (1988) proposes a **verbal shell** structure. In the following, the empty head is a place holder and has no independent semantic import.

(71) $[_{VP}$ SU $[_{V'}$ e $[_{VP}$ DO $[_{V'}$ V IO$]]]]$

(72)

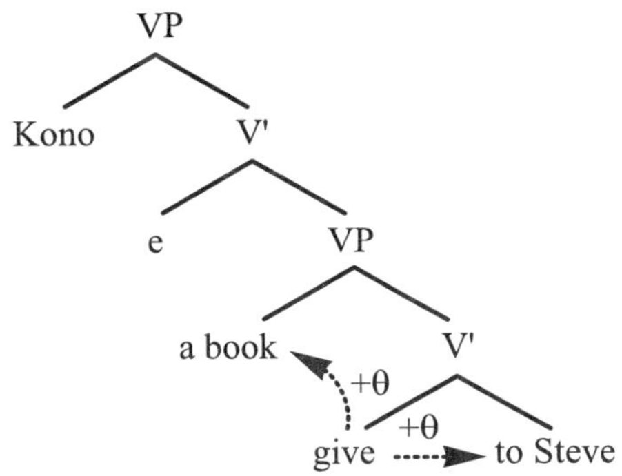

The thematic V moves to the position of the empty V in order to **discharge** the external **θ-role**.

(73)

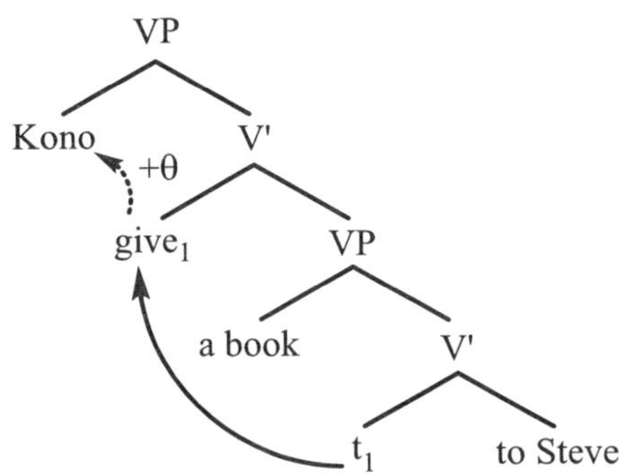

Given this, one potential argument **against DS** can be formulated; all θ-roles are not always discharged at DS. This is a welcoming result for Minimalism, which attempts to eliminate DS and SS out of Grammar.

Exercise 3

《3-1》

Discuss the evidence of postulating a trace. (Do not exceed the length of 20 lines.)

《3-2》

Compare the Projection Principle and the Extended Projection Principle (EPP). (Do not exceed the length of 10 lines.)

《3-3》

Explain why the θ-criterion should be formulated being conjunctive: each argument bears one and only one θ-role, and each θ-role is assigned to one and only one argument. (Do not exceed the length of 20 lines.)

《3-4》

Discuss the idiom argument for the PISH. (Do not exceed the length of 10 lines.)

《3-5》

Discuss the CSC argument for the PISH. (Do not exceed the length of 10 lines.)

《3-6》

Discuss the binding argument for the PISH. (Do not exceed the length of 10 lines.)

《3-7》

Discuss the floating quantifier argument for the PISH. (Do not exceed the length of 10 lines.)

《3-8》

Discuss the word order argument for the PISH. (Do not exceed the length of 10 lines.)

《3-9》

Discuss what the derivational θ-marking is. (Do not exceed the length of 20 lines.)

Robert May

http://philosophy.ucdavis.edu/people/rcmay

- Expertise: Philosophy of Language and Logic, History of Early Analytic Philosophy, Theoretical Linguistics, Syntax and Semantics, etc.
- Institutions: University of California at Davis (since 2006), University of California at Irvine (1986-2006)
- Degree: MIT (PhD)
- Doctoral Advisor: Noam Chomsky
- Dissertation Title: *The Grammar of Quantification* (1977)
- Known for: Antecedent-Contained Deletion, Ellipsis, Logical Form, Quantifier Raising, Vehicle Change, etc.

4 Move α

There are two types of rules in Grammar: **PS rules** and **Transformational rules** (= Transformations). Phrase markers (= P-markers = PS trees = Trees) are formed based on PS rules. Transformations convert a P-marker (e.g., DS tree) into another P-marker (e.g., SS tree).

4.1 Transformational Operations

There are three elementary transformational **operations** in Generative Grammar: substitution, adjunction, and deletion.

Substitution is a **structure-preserving** operation that replaces one category with another category as long as the two categories are non-distinct. There are two types of substitution: movement substitution and insertion substitution.

(1) a. movement substitution b. insertion substitution

Adjunction is a **structure-building** operation. It creates a new hierarchical structure in a P-marker.

(2) a. left adjunction b. right adjunction

Deletion is an operation which makes some constituent invisible (i.e., unpronounced) from the structure. It observes a **recoverability condition** in the sense that a constituent cannot be deleted without being recovered from a linguistic or situational antecedent.

(3)

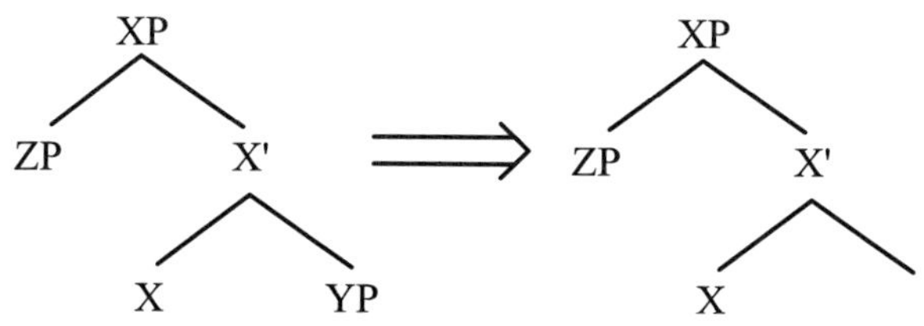

The direct question in (4a) involves three kinds of movement, as illustrated in (4b). The progressive Aux, inserting into a higher V and then adjoining to I, adjoins to C—an instance of head movement. Under the PISH, the VP-internal subject substitutes into Spec of IP—an instance of A-movement. The interrogative pronoun object of the preposition substitutes into Spec of CP—an instance of A'-movement.

(4) a. What is Barney working on?

b. [$_{CP}$ what$_1$ [$_{C'}$ [wh]$_C$-[pres]$_I$-be$_2$ [$_{IP}$ Barney$_3$ [$_{I'}$ t$_2$ [$_{VP}$ t$_2$ [$_{VP}$ t$_3$ working on t$_1$]]]]]]

Subject raising is an instance of **substitution**. As illustrated in (5), the subject of the complement clause of *seem* should be raised to the matrix subject position when the complement is infinitival, and should not when the complement clause is finite as in (6).

(5) a. *It seems [the situation to be getting worse].

b. The situation$_1$ seems [t$_1$ to be getting worse]. MOVEMENT

(6) a. It seems that the situation is getting worse. INSERTION

b. *The situation$_1$ seems [(that) t$_1$ is getting worse].

The matrix subject position is empty at DS. As (5) and (6) show, there are two options for filling this position: inserting a pleonastic element or moving an element from some other position.

In (7) a relative clause (CP) is **extraposed** to VP via an **adjunction**.

(7) [$_{DP}$ An article on particle theory t$_1$] [$_{VP}$ [$_{VP}$ just appeared]
[$_{CP}$ which I want to read]$_1$].

Substitution movements and **adjunction** movements are grouped under the umbrella of **Move α**, where α stands for any category. That is, Move α refers to the generalized transformation, licensing any types of movement. The well-formedness of each movement is decided by the interaction of Grammar **modules**.

(8) Move α

Move (i.e., substitute or adjoin) anything anywhere.

It is assumed in Chomsky (*LGB*) that Move α does not contain a deletion operation since the latter is structure-destroying. Move α leaves behind a trace of the moving element.

Lasnik and Saito (1984, 1992) argue that traces need not be left by movement unless their presence is mandatory for independent rules or principles. They point out that deletion operations are not limited to the derivation between SS and PF, and so need not be considered independently of substitution and adjunction. Therefore, **elementary operations** might be unified under the single rubric of **Affect α**.

(9) Affect α

Affect (i.e., substitute, adjoin, or delete) anything anywhere.

In GB, a chain is created as the result of movement. The moved element is the head of the chain, and the original trace is the tail/foot of the chain. Argument chains (**A-chains**) have a θ-role and Case, and must comply with the **Chain Condition**. In (11) a four-member chain is illustrated.

(10) The Chain Condition

A well-formed A-chain must contain one θ-marked position and one Case-marked position.

(11)	Chain = (α,	t'',	t',	t)
	HEAD			TAIL/FOOT
	+CASE			+θ

Apparently, (12a) seems to have one chain with three-members, as shown in (12c). In fact, however, it has two separate chains, as shown in (13). The A-chain in (13a) is created by the A-movement of *who* from the object position of *kissed* to Spec of IP. The A'-chain in (13b) is created by the A'-movement of *who* from Spec of IP to Spec of CP. In this case, the A-movement feeds the A'-movement.

(12) a. Who was kissed?

b. ______ was kissed who — DS

c. $[_{CP}$ who$_1$ $[_{IP}$ t'$_1$ was kissed t$_1$]] — SS

A'-POS A-POS A-POS

+CASE +θ

(13) a. A-chain = (t'$_1$, t$_1$)

b. A'-chain = (who$_1$, t'$_1$)

There are three types of movement transformations, depending on the **types of moving elements**.

(14) a. A-movement

b. A'-movement

c. Head Movement

4.2 A-movement

Passivization is an instance of A-movement.♣

(15) a. ___ was amended the contract — DS

b. The contract$_1$ was amended t$_1$. — SS

Baker (1997) proposes the Uniformity θ-role Assignment Hypothesis (**UTAH**):♣♣

(16) The Uniformity θ-role Assignment Hypothesis (UTAH)

Arguments which bear the same θ-role are generated in the same DS position.

Given the UTAH, compare (17a) and (17b). Theme arguments are assumed to originate uniformly in the complement position of a verb.

♣ See section 7.3.2.

♣♣ The UTAH demands the direct mapping between θ-roles and structural positions. Thus, Agent is necessarily structurally higher than Theme and Location, according to the Thematic Hierarchy.

(i) The Thematic Hierarchy

Agent/Causer >

Theme/Patient >

Path/Location

(17) a. The lawyer amended the contract.
THEME

b. The contract was amended ___ by the lawyer.
THEME

Middle constructions show a case of A-movement.♣

(18) These potatoes mash well.

DS (19) a. ___ mash these potatoes well

SS b. These potatoes$_1$ mash t$_1$ well.

Ergative (= unaccusative) constructions show a case of A-movement as in (20a). In (20b) the expletive *there* is inserted into Spec of IP in order to satisfy the subject requirement in English (i.e., the EPP), instead of A-movement.

(20) a. A party of linguists$_1$ arrived t$_1$.

b. cf. There arrived a party of linguists.

Unergatives may select cognate objects.

(21) a. He died a terrible death.

b. He smiled a rueful smile.

c. He danced a merry dance.

In a sense, ergatives and transitives are similar in that they cannot tolerate cognate objects. In this light, it could be assumed that ergative Vs are a type of transitive Vs.

(22) a. *He arrived an arrival.

b. *They destroyed a destruction.

Raising is a case of A-movement.♣♣

DS (23) a. ___ seems [Steve to have lost his passport]

SS b. Steve$_1$ seems [t$_1$ to have lost his passport].

♣ See section 7.3.3.

♣♣ See section 7.3.1.

Control is not a case of A-movement, as shown in (24b).♣

(24) a. Steve$_1$ seems t_1 to have lost his passport.
b. Steve$_1$ expects PRO$_1$ to have lost his passport.

The following is synonymous with (24a).

(25) It seems that Steve has lost his passport.

Compare (24b) with the following:

(26) *It expects that Steve has lost his passport.

Thus, the **Argument Structures** of raising Vs and control Vs should be different.

(27) a. seem: [___ CP] <THEME>
b. expect: [___ CP] <EXPERIENCER, THEME>

The VP-internal subject movement is a case of A-movement.

(28) a. ___ will [the princess kiss the frog] DS
b. The princess$_1$ will [t_1 kiss the frog]. SS

Note that an adjunct DP cannot move into the subject position. Why? By assumption, it does not have N-feature (i.e., EPP feature or categorial D-feature) to satisfy the Subject Requirement (i.e., the EPP) in English.

(29) a. The lawyer amended the contract last night.
*Last night was amended the contract.
b. We mashed the potatoes well every time.
*Every time mash the potatoes well.
c. There arrived a package last week.
*Last week arrived a package.
d. It seems that each day Steve loses his passport.
*Each day seems Steve to lose his passport.

♣ See chapter 10 for an extensive discussion of control.

To summarize, the following is an instance of A-movement: passivization, middle constructions, ergative/unaccusative constructions, raising, and subject movement.

4.3 A'-movement

The following illustrates an instance of wh-movement, head movement, and DP movement.

(30) a. Which contract has the lawyer amended?

DS b. the lawyer has amended which contract

SS c. [$_{CP}$ which contract$_1$ [$_{C'}$ has$_2$ [$_{IP}$ the lawyer$_3$ [$_{I'}$ t'$_2$ [$_{VP}$ t$_2$ [$_{VP}$ t$_3$ amended t$_1$]]]]]]

APs and PPs can undergo wh-movement.

(31) a. How bad did the news seem?

b. By whom was the murder victim discovered?

Adjuncts can undergo wh-movement.

(32) a. When did the maid change the linen?

b. For how long was the miscalculation kept from the public?

Wh-movement is an instance of A'-movement. The target for wh-movement is an A'-position (e.g., Spec of CP).

Topicalization is an instance of A'-movement. Under the standard assumption, the target for topicalization is an IP-adjoined position.

(33) I thought that *this exam*, everyone would pass.

Negative-fronting is an instance of A'-movement. The target for negative-fronting could be Spec of CP or Spec of a functional category.

(34) *Never again* will he chase his kids down a beach.

In some languages like Korean, wh-interpretation doesn't have to be realized with overt wh-movement. That is, **wh-in situ** is possible.

(35) [$_{CP}$ What$_1$ do [you want t$_1$]]?

(36)

너는	무엇을	원하니?
Ne-nun	**mwues**-ul	weonha-ni?
you-Top	what-Acc	want-Q

'What do you want?'

French allows both wh-fronting and wh-in situ.

(37) a.

Qu'	est	que	tu	veux?
What	is	that	you	want

'What do you want?'

b.

Tu	veux	**quois**?
you	want	what

To summarize, the following is an instance of A'-movement: wh-movement, topicalization, and negative-fronting.

4.4 Head Movement

The following shows a way of deriving *yes/no* questions from the declarative counterparts. The transformation involved is called Subject-Aux Inversion (**SAI**).

(38) a. Kono is leaving for Paris tomorrow.
→ Is Kono leaving for Paris tomorrow?

b. Kono has been to Paris before.
→ Has Kono been to Paris before?

c. Kono can afford this trip.
→ Can Kono afford this trip?

According to **Standard Theory** (Chomsky *Aspects*), a surface tree of (38a) is as follows:

(39)

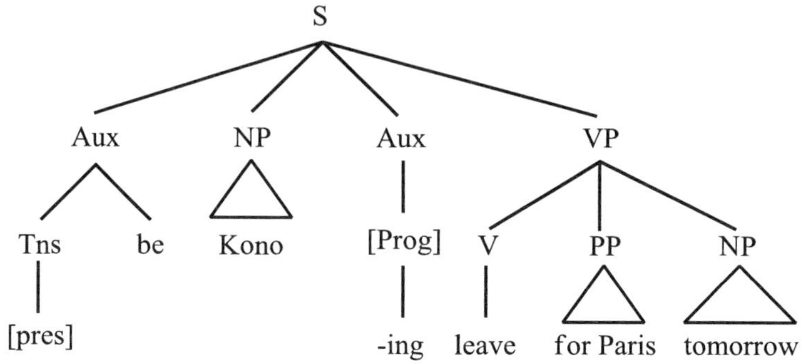

The following shows that **negative statements** are derived, via inserting *not*, from the corresponding positive statements in (38).

(40) a. Kono is not leaving for Paris tomorrow.
b. Kono has not been to Paris before.
c. Kono cannot afford this trip.

The **contraction** of *not* to *-n't* is allowed. This contraction is optional in declarative contexts.

(41) a. Kono isn't leaving for Paris tomorrow.
b. Kono hasn't been to Paris before.
c. Kono can't afford this trip.

The following shows the formation of **negative questions** from those of (41).

(42) a. Isn't Kono leaving tomorrow?
b. Hasn't Kono been to Paris before?
c. Can't Kono afford this trip?

What is interesting is that the contraction in negative question contexts is **forced**. Observe the ungrammaticality of (43). A question is then why. One plausible answer is that there is only one head position, C, outside of IP.

(43) a. *Is not Kono leaving tomorrow?
b. *Has not Kono been to Paris before?
c. *Cannot Kono afford this trip?

Note that it is possible to leave the negative element behind.

(44) a. Is Kono not leaving tomorrow?
b. Has Kono not been to Paris before?
c. Can Kono not afford this trip?

We cannot put an auxiliary and a complementizer in the same position. Why? The same answer can be provided; there is only one head position, C, outside of IP.

(45) A: What did the journalist from the *Washington Post* ask you?
B: *If was the president lying.

How is it possible that an auxiliary like *was* is placed in the head C position of CP? An auxiliary in INFL is allowed to move to C.

(46) a. Was Barney lying?
b. [$_{CP}$ ___ [$_{IP}$ ___ [$_{I'}$ past [$_{VP}$ be [$_{VP}$ Barney lying]]]]] DS
c. [$_{CP}$ was$_2$ [$_{IP}$ Barney$_1$ [$_{I'}$ t'$_2$ [$_{VP}$ t$_2$ [$_{VP}$ t$_1$ lying]]]]] SS

Consider the following:

(47) He asked [$_{CP}$ whether we would return].

The SAI in an embedded CP that includes a complementizer is not grammatical:

(48) *He asked [$_{CP}$ whether would$_1$ we t$_1$ return].

The SAI in an embedded CP that does not have a complementizer is acceptable in some **dialects**. A consequence is that a complementizer such as *whether* and an inverted auxiliary such as *would* occupy the same position, C.

(49) He asked [$_{CP}$ would$_1$ we t$_1$ return].

Consider the following contrast in English:

(50) a. Paul always works.
b. *Paul works always.

Let's compare English and French. If an adverb precedes the verb in French, the sentence is ungrammatical. If an adverb follows the verb, the sentence is grammatical:

(51)	a.	*Paul	toujours	travaille.
		Paul	always	works
		'Paul always works.'		
	b.	Paul	travaille	toujours.
		Paul	works	always

An **Aux V** is inverted (i.e., I-to-C movement) in **English** interrogative sentences. But a non-Aux V is not.

(52) a. Will you t stay for supper?
b. *Stay you t for supper?

Both **Aux Vs** and **non-Aux Vs** are inverted in **French** interrogative sentences.

(53)	As$_1$-tu	t$_1$	essayé?
	have-you		tried
	'Have you tried?'		

(54) Vois$_1$-tu t_1 le livre?
see you the book
'Do you see the book?'

Consider the interaction of V-raising (i.e., V-to-I movement) and Inversion (i.e., I-to-C movement) in French below:

(55) a. V-raising
[$_{CP}$ Q [$_{IP}$ tu$_1$ vois$_2$ [$_{VP}$ t_1 t_2 le livre]]]

b. Inversion
[$_{CP}$ Q-vois$_2$ [$_{IP}$ tu$_1$ t'$_2$ [$_{VP}$ t_1 t_2 le livre]]]

Non-modal Auxes are considered to be a special type of **V** that takes a VP complement.

(56) a. The children should$_I$ [$_{VP}$ have$_V$ [$_{VP}$ waited$_V$]].
b. Those guys may$_I$ [$_{VP}$ be$_V$ [$_{VP}$ sleeping$_V$]].

Consider the following tree bracketing containing two Aux Vs. The first Aux resides in INFL, and the second one in a higher V.

(57) [$_{IP}$ The children$_1$ [$_{I'}$ should [$_{VP}$ have [$_{VP}$ t_1 waited]]]].

As expected, only the modal Aux can undergo Inversion in (57). If the non-modal Aux moves to the C position, the Head Movement Constraint (HMC) or Minimality is violated.

(58) a. [$_{CP}$ Should [$_{IP}$ the children t have waited]]?

b. *[$_{CP}$ Have [$_{IP}$ the children should t waited]]?

A **non-modal Aux** can undergo Inversion when there is no modal Aux in the sentence.

(59) a. The children have waited for two hours.
b. $Have_1$ the children t_1 waited for two hours?

English main Vs never move to the C position. ***Do* insertion** is needed for English verbal morphology.

(60) a. *Arrived they ___ on time?
b. Did they ___ arrive on time?

French main Vs behave like **Auxes** by moving to a sentence-initial position.

(61) a. Avez-vous chanté dans la classe?
have you sung in the class
'Have you sung in the class?'
b. Chantez-vous bien?
sing you well
'Do you sing well?'

Recall that English aspectual Auxes such as *have* or *be* are generated in their own VP projection as they are not in complementary distribution with modal Auxes and so are not generated in INFL.

(62) a. I $should_I$ [$_{VP}$ never [$_{VP}$ $have_V$ [$_{VP}$ met him]]].
b. I had_I [$_{VP}$ never [$_{VP}$ t_V [$_{VP}$ met him]]].

French Vs can **move** to I **overtly**.♣

(63) Jean embrasse souvent Marie.
John kisses often Mary
'John often kisses Mary.'

♣ Note that the AdvP in (64) is assumed to adjoin to VP.

(64)

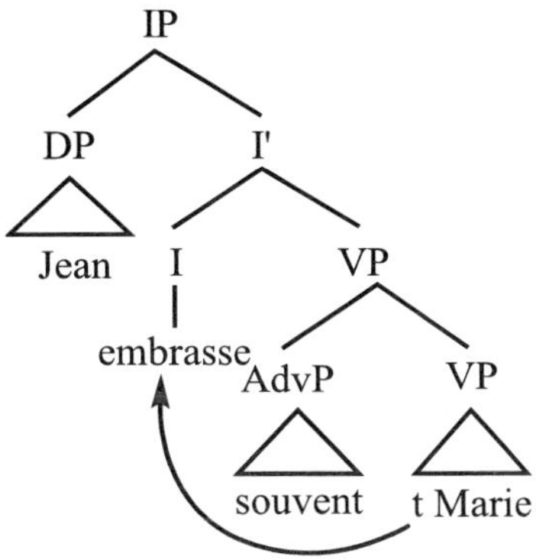

This is not possible in English.

(65) a. *John kisses often Mary.
b. John often kisses Mary.

English does not have overt V-raising. Instead, it has **affix hopping** (= affix lowering) in order to form verbal morphology (Chomsky *SynStrs*).♣

(66) [$_{IP}$ John$_1$ [pres] [$_{VP}$ t$_1$ often kiss Mary]].

To summarize, SAI (= I-to-C movement) and French verb movement (= V-to-I movement) are instances of head movement.

♣ Alternatively, the verbal morphology in English could be formed via PF merger.

Exercise 4

《 4-1 》

Compare the following elementary transformational operations: substitution, adjunction, and deletion. (Do not exceed the length of 15 lines.)

《 4-2 》

Compare Move α and Affect α. (Do not exceed the length of 20 lines.)

《 4-3 》

What is the Chain Condition? (Do not exceed the length of 10 lines.)

《 4-4 》

What is the Uniformity θ-role Assignment Hypothesis (UTAH)? (Do not exceed the length of 10 lines.)

《 4-5 》

What is A-movment? Provide at least five different kinds of A-movement. (Do not exceed the length of 20 lines.)

《 4-6 》

What is A'-movment? Provide at least three different kinds of A'-movement. (Do not exceed the length of 20 lines.)

《 4-7 》

What is head movement? Provide at least two different kinds of head movement. (Do not exceed the length of 20 lines.)

Government Theory

Government is a type of dependency relation in which an element decides the grammatical function (GF) of another elements and selects its morphological properties.

5.1 Empty Categories

Empty categories are not totally empty. They don't have phonological import but have syntactic and semantic import. Standardly, there are four empty categories such as little pro, big PRO, DP-trace (DP-t) and wh-trace (wh-t).

Pro refers to an empty subject in pro-drop languages such as Spanish. It doesn't exist in (standard) English.

(1) **pro** Te quiero.
you want-1st person
'I want you.'

PRO is an unpronounced pronoun which plays the role of a subject in nonfinite clauses.

(2) Ted$_1$ prefers PRO$_1$ to invite Robin.

DP movement leaves a **DP-t**.

(3) Adam$_1$ is loved t$_1$ by Kono.

Wh-movement leaves a **wh-t**.

(4) What$_1$ did Steve eat t$_1$?

If there is long-distance wh-movement, more than one wh-t may be created. In (5) the wh-t in the embedded Spec of CP is called an **intermediate wh-t**, which is created by syntactic purposes (i.e., Shortest Move). Since it does not contribute to the meaning of a sentence, it may be subject to LF deletion (via Affect α). However, the original wh-t is significant in LF for interpretation. It hosts both a θ-role and Case. This original wh-t is called a **variable**.

(5) What$_1$ do you think [$_{CP}$ t'$_1$ [$_{IP}$ Steve ate t$_1$]]?

Empty categories have the same features as their phonetic counterparts. The following is the typology of empty categories.

(6)

COVERT	OVERT	TYPE
DP-t	anaphors	[+anaphor, -pronominal]
pro	pronouns	[-anaphor, +pronominal]
variable	R-expressions	[-anaphor, -pronominal]
PRO	___	[+anaphor, +pronominal]

5.2 Complement vs. Non-complement Asymmetry

The core part of **Government Theory** is the **Empty Category Principle (ECP)**, which determines the distribution of traces created by Move α.

(7) The Empty Category Principle (ECP)

Traces must be properly governed.

Proper Government is a more restrictive version of government. **Lexical heads** are proper governors but functional heads are not.

(8) α **properly governs** β if and only if

a. α **governs** β and

b. α is **lexical** or an **antecedent**.

The following long-distance wh-movement illustrates the so-called **subject-object asymmetry**.

(9) a. [$_{CP}$ Who$_1$ does [$_{IP}$ Kono believe [$_{CP}$ t_1 that [$_{IP}$ Danny [$_{VP}$ admires t_1]]]]]?

(intermediate t_1: -LG, +AG; object t_1: +LG, +AG)

b. *[$_{CP}$ Who$_1$ does [$_{IP}$ Kono believe [$_{CP}$ t_1 that [$_{IP}$ t_1 [$_{VP}$ admires Danny]]]]]?

(intermediate t_1: -LG, +AG; subject t_1: -LG, -AG)

With respect to proper government, the wh-movement from an object position is always licensed by a lexical verb, whereas that from a subject position is not. Note that the object trace is lexically governed, whereas the subject trace is not. Thus, **lexical government** provides one way of satisfying the ECP.

If the ECP is a constraint on every trace, the intermediate trace in (9a) should be licensed by another mechanism since it is not lexically governed. This mechanism is called **antecedent government**. In (9a) *who* antecedent-governs its trace in the embedded Spec of CP.

Even if **intermediate traces** were excluded from the ECP requirement, some notion of antecedent government would be indispensable for

(10), where the subject trace is not lexically governed:

(10) a. Who$_1$ did [$_{IP}$ Kono say [$_{CP}$ t$_1$ [$_{IP}$ t$_1$ [$_{VP}$ admires Danny]]]]?
-LG
+AG

b. *It is disturbing [the situation$_1$ to be reported [$_{XP}$ t$_1$ is getting worse]].
BA -LG
-AG

(cf. It is disturbing (that) it has been reported that the situation is getting worse.)

The grammaticality of (10a) suggests that the subject trace should be antecedent-governed since it is not lexically governed by either the matrix verb or the embedded verb. The ungrammaticality of (10b) suggests that the subject trace is neither lexically nor antecedent-governed. The XP, whether it is a CP or IP boundary, constitutes a barrier to proper government.

To summarize, it appears that the ECP is **disjunctive** in that it is satisfied either by lexical or antecedent government.

The examples in (11) are deviant, given that the fronted wh-phrases are extracted out of the infinitival clauses, respectively. According to Ross's islands, both (11a) and (11b) violate the Wh-island Constraint.

*SUBJACENCY, *ECP
*SUBJACENCY, √ECP

(11) a. *How are you wondering [which car to fix]?
b. ?*Which car are you wondering [how to fix]?

Of particular interest is that the deviancy of (11a) is worse than that of (11b). This difference is captured by an ECP analysis, given the representations (12a) and (12b), respectively:

(12) a. *[$_{CP}$ how$_2$ are [$_{IP}$ you wondering [$_{CP}$ which car$_1$ [$_{IP}$ PRO to [$_{VP}$ fix t$_1$] t$_2$]]]]]
+LG -LG
+AG -AG

b. ?*[$_{CP}$ which car$_1$ are [$_{IP}$ you wondering [$_{CP}$ how$_2$ [$_{IP}$ PRO to [$_{VP}$ fix t$_1$] t$_2$]]]]
+LG -LG
-AG +AG

Both (12a) and (12b) violate the Subjacency Condition because the sentence-initial wh-phrases have moved over two bounding nodes (i.e., the two IPs). (12a) in particular violates the ECP because the trace of *how* is neither lexically nor antecedent-governed. In (12b) the trace of *which car* is lexically governed, and the trace of *how* is antecedent-governed, thus satisfying the ECP.

5.3 Barriers

The potential barrierhood of the matrix VP as a **blocking category** (defined as a category that is not L-marked) should be nullified for long-distance movement. Kayne (1989) suggests that an auxiliary verb L-marks VP. Chomsky (*Barriers*) proposes that a wh-phrase adjoins to VP on its way to the matrix CP (resulting in 13), assuming that **adjunction** structures do **not** constitute **barriers**. (Irrelevant parts are suppressed.)

(13) [$_{CP}$ Who$_1$ did [$_{IP}$ Kono [$_{VP}$ t$_1$ [$_{VP}$ say [$_{CP}$ t$_1$ [$_{IP}$ t$_1$ [$_{VP}$ admires Danny]]]]]]]?

Let's assume that the XP in (10b), repeated below as (14), is CP. In contrast to (10a), the CP in (14) constitutes a barrier. That is, the subject trace (t$_1$) in the lowest clause violates the ECP. Although the complement CP is L-marked by a higher predicate (*reported*), it is counted as an inherited barrier since it dominates the blocking category IP.

(14) *It is disturbing [the situation$_1$ to be reported
[$_{CP}$ [$_{IP}$ t$_1$ is getting worse]]].
BC BC -LG
BA -AG

In (12a), an SS representation of (11a), the complement CP becomes a barrier regarding the adjunct movement of *how*. Under the barriers analysis, (11a) would be represented as in (15), where both wh-phrases have moved via adjunction to VP. In (15) the complement CP becomes an inherited barrier due to dominating the embedded IP, a blocking category. (Irrelevant parts are suppressed.)

(15) *[$_{CP}$ How$_2$ are [$_{IP}$ you [$_{VP}$ t$_2$ [$_{VP}$ wondering] [$_{CP}$ which car$_1$ [$_{IP}$
ADJUNCTION BA BC
PRO to [$_{VP}$ t$_2$ [$_{VP}$ t$_1$ [$_{VP}$ fix]] t$_2$]]]]]]?
ADJUNCTION

To account for the ***that*-trace effect** in (9b), Chomsky introduces the Minimality Condition.

(16) The **Minimality Condition** (Chomsky *Barriers*: 42)
In ... α ... [$_{\gamma}$ ... δ ... β ...] ..., α does not govern β if γ is a projection of δ excluding α.♣

The example in (9b) meets the structural description of the Minimality Condition, as illustrated in (17), where β = the trace in IP, δ = the complementizer *that*, γ = C', and α = the trace in CP.

(17) [$_{CP}$ t'$_1$ [$_{C'}$ that [$_{IP}$ t$_1$ ...
-AG

The notion of barriers is proposed to unify the **ECP** and the **Subjacency** Condition. Example (18) violates the Subjacency Condition but observes the ECP as follows:

*SUBJACENCY, √ECP

(18) *The politician [$_{CP}$ who$_1$ [$_{IP}$ [$_{DP}$ an article by t$_1$] appeared in the
BC BC +LG
BA BA -AG
Washington Post]] is energetic.

♣ A narrower formulation of the Minimality Condition adds the following requirement: γ immediately dominates β.

Both the IP and DP in (18) are not L-marked, thus being blocking categories. Thus, the DP becomes an inherent barrier, and the IP becomes an inherited barrier due to dominating the blocking category DP. The wh-movement crosses two barriers in violation of Subjacency. Note that the trace satisfies the ECP because it is lexically governed by the preposition *by*.♣

5.4 Superiority

In English **multiple wh-questions**, only one wh-phrase moves overtly.

(19) a. $[_{CP}$ Who$_1$ $[_{IP}$ t_1 saw what]]?
b. $[_{CP}$ How$_1$ did $[_{IP}$ they travel where t_1]]?

(20) a. *What who saw?
b. *Who what saw?

(21) a. *How where did they travel?
b. *Where how did they travel?

Multiple wh-questions often solicit multiple-pair answers. For example, (19a) could be answered as (22).

(22) Steve saw a black car draw up, Danny saw a shadowy figure enter the house, and Kono saw someone running down the drive.

A question is then why the **unmoved** wh-element, the wh-in situ, is still interpreted as an **interrogative operator**. One plausible answer in the literature is to assume that the unmoved wh-elements in multiple questions undergo covert wh-movement to Spec of CP.♣♣

In some cases, insofar as one wh-element moves overtly, and the other stays in situ, either wh-element is allowed to move overtly.

(23) a. I wonder which wine Ann bought for whom.
b. I wonder for whom Ann bought which wine.

♣ See also section 6.4 for further discussion of *barriers*.

♣♣ In echo questions, wh-elements do not move overtly. The in-situ wh-elements in echo questions are interpreted differently from those in normal wh-questions. The former is interpreted as being more specific than the latter. That is, they act as information triggers for misheard facts or data.
(i) a. You saw what?
b. They traveled where?

In others, however, only the superior wh-element is allowed to move overtly. Note that the subject wh-element is higher than the object wh-element.

(24) a. I wonder [$_{CP}$ who$_1$ [$_{IP}$ t$_1$ bought what]].
b. *I wonder [$_{CP}$ what$_1$ [$_{IP}$ who bought t$_1$]].

Given the ***Barriers*** formulations of the **ECP** and **Subjacency**, there might be a potential contradiction if both apply at the same level of representation. In fact, there is evidence that the Subjacency Condition holds at SS, while the ECP had better apply at LF.

An LF analysis of the ECP is motivated by Superiority effects as in (24) or (25):

(25) a. [$_{CP}$ Who$_1$ [$_{IP}$ t$_1$ [$_{VP}$ wrote what]]]?
b. *[$_{CP}$ What$_1$ did [$_{IP}$ who [$_{VP}$ write t$_1$]]]?

In (25) the subject *who* was higher than the object *what* at DS in that the former asymmetrically c-commands the latter. In the generative tradition, Chomsky (1973) proposed the **Superiority Condition** according to which an element cannot cross over a higher element of the same type via a transformation. In GB, it was possible to subsume the Superiority effects if the ECP holds at LF.

The LF wh-movement results in the **adjunction** of the overtly in-situ wh-phrase to the fronted wh-phrase in Spec of CP. This process is referred to as **absorption** (Higginbotham and May 1981). Of the resulting LF representations of (25), (26a) satisfies the ECP, but (26b) violates it:

√ECP (26) a. [$_{CP}$ [What$_2$ who$_1$]$_1$ [$_{IP}$ t$_1$ [$_{VP}$ wrote t$_2$]]]?
t$_1$: -LG, +AG; t$_2$: +LG, -AG

*ECP b. *[$_{CP}$ [Who$_2$ what$_1$]$_1$ did [$_{IP}$ t$_2$ [$_{VP}$ write t$_1$]]]?
t$_2$: -LG, -AG; t$_1$: +LG, +AG

In (26a) the trace of *what* is lexically governed, and the trace of *who* is antecedent-governed. In (26b), however, the trace of *what* is both lexically governed and antecedent-governed, while the trace of *who* is neither. In particular, antecedent government between *who* and its trace fails because the wh-phrase does not bind its trace.

Exercise 5

《5-1》

How many types of empty categories are there in Generative Grammar? (Do not exceed the length of 20 lines.)

《5-2》

Explain what the subject-object asymmetry is, illustrating an example. (Do not exceed the length of 20 lines.)

《5-3》

Why is the ECP formulated as being disjunctive in Chomksy (*LGB*)? (Do not exceed the length of 20 lines.)

《5-4》

Why does a wh-phrase move overtly to the target via VP adjunction in Chomsky (*Barriers*)? (Do not exceed the length of 20 lines.)

《5-5》

What is the use of the Minimality Condition? (Do not exceed the length of 10 lines.)

《5-6》

What is the Superiority effect? How is it accounted for by the ECP? (Do not exceed the length of 20 lines.)

《5-7》

Explain the process of Higginbotham and May's (1981) absorption. (Do not exceed the length of 10 lines.)

6

Bounding Theory

Grammatical movements should be shortest as a consequence of restrictions imposed directly on movement by the independent module of Bounding Theory.

6.1 A-over-A

The **A-over-A** Principle is a universal constraint on transformational operations suggested by Chomsky (1964). The principle states that if there are two phrases of the same category, both of which are possible targets of a particular operation and if one phrase contains the other, then it is the maximal phrase that the operation applies to.

For example, consider the following coordinated structures. This principle prevents extraction of the lower DP out of the higher DP in which it is included as in (1b), but allows the more **inclusive** DP to be fronted as in (1c).♣

(1) a. We have to read [$_{DP}$ [$_{DP}$ some books] and [$_{DP}$ some papers]].

b. *Which books$_1$ do we have to read [$_{DP}$ [$_{DP}$ t$_1$] and [$_{DP}$ some papers]]?

♣ Criticism of this principle in later developments of transformational grammar can be found in Ross (1967). Much later, the A-over-A principle has been reduced to principles such as the ECP (Chomsky *LGB*, *Barriers*).

c. $[_{DP}$ $[_{DP}$ Which books] and $[_{DP}$ which papers$]]_1$ do we have to read t_1?

(2)

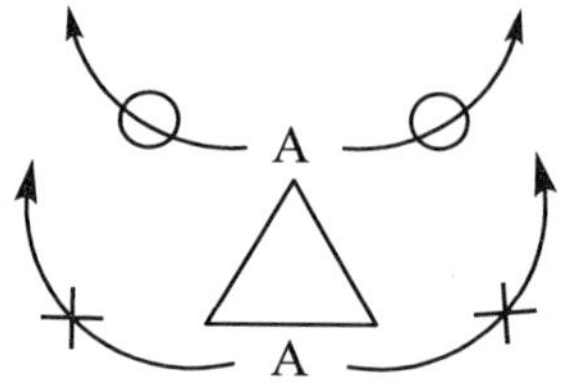

In short, the Coordinated Structure Constraint (CSC) violation is explained by the A-over-A Principle.

6.2 Islands

Several island constraints or conditions are proposed to capture the boundedness effects of long-distance movement (cf. Ross 1967).

Extraction out of embedded clauses introduced by wh-elements is deviant. The following violates the **Wh-island Constraint**.

(3) a. *Who$_1$ did he ask [when she saw t_1]?
b. *What$_2$ did Ann wonder [who$_1$ t_1 would eat t_2]?
c. *Who$_2$ did David ask [who$_1$ t_1 fired t_2]?

No extraction is possible out of complex nominal domains such as noun-complement clauses or relative clauses. The Complex Noun Phrase Constraint (**CNPC**) blocks wh-movement out of an NP/DP island.

(4) a. *Who$_1$ did he hear [the rumor that she murdered t_1]?
b. *Which exam$_1$ did you talk to [a girl {who, that} passed t_1]?

No extraction is possible out of sentential subject domains. The following violates the Sentential Subject Constraint (**SSC**).

(5) *Who$_1$ was$_2$ [that you met t$_1$] t$_2$ unexpected?

No extraction is possible out of subject DP domains. The following violates the Subject Condition (**SC**).

(6) *Who$_1$ did [a picture of t$_1$] fall off the wall?

No extraction is possible out of adjunct domains. The following violates the Adjunct Condition (**AC**).♣

(7) *Who$_1$ did he leave [because he met t$_1$]?

Extraction is not possible out of coordinate structures unless it happens in an ATB manner out of every conjunct. The following violates the Coordinate Structure Constraint (**CSC**).

(8) a. *Which books$_1$ do we have to read [t$_1$ and some papers]?
b. *That book$_1$, I like [this magazine and t$_1$].

The left branch of nominals cannot be extracted. The following violates the Left Branching Condition (**LBC**).

(9) *Whose$_1$ did she like [t$_1$ top-siders]?

Rightward extraction out of a clause is banned. Example (10b) violates the Right Roof Constraint (**RRC**).

(10) a. The fact [that Ross gave t$_1$ to Joey the books which my uncle left to me$_1$] is of no consequence.
b. *The fact [that Ross gave t$_1$ to Joey] is of no consequence the books which my uncle left to me$_1$.

However, Islands are not explanatory, just being descriptive.

♣ The SC and the AC can collapse into Huang's (1982) Condition on Extraction Domain (CED). According to the CED, no extraction is possible out of non-complement domains such as subject domains or adjunct domains.

6.3 Subjacency

Long-distance movement should be made in short hops rather than in one fell swoop hop. The Wh-island violation in (11b) and Superraising in (12b) are ruled out since each long-distance movement is forced for independent reasons.

(11) a. $[_{CP}$ Who$_1$ did $[_{IP}$ he think $[_{CP}$ t$_1$ $[_{IP}$ she saw t$_1$]]]]?

*WH-ISLAND b. *$[_{CP}$ Who$_1$ did $[_{IP}$ he ask $[_{CP}$ when $[_{IP}$ she saw t$_1$]]]]?

(12) a. $[_{IP}$ He$_1$ seems $[_{IP}$ t$_1$ to be likely $[_{IP}$ t$_1$ to leave]]].

SUPERRAISING b. *$[_{IP}$ He$_1$ seems $[_{CP}$ that $[_{IP}$ it is likely $[_{IP}$ t$_1$ to leave]]]].

Movement operations are bounded within a particular syntactic domain. There is a condition on movement called the **Subjacency Condition**, which can accommodate the Wh-island effect and the Superraising effect.

(13) No movement can cross more than one bounding node (e.g., IP or DP).

The contrast in (14) provides additional illustration of bounding phenomena.

(14) a. $[_{DP}$ An author of $[_{DP}$ an article on particle theory] t$_1$] $[_{VP}$ $[_{VP}$ just arrived] $[_{CP}$ who I want to meet]$_1$].

b. *$[_{DP}$ An author of $[_{DP}$ an article on particle theory t$_1$]] $[_{VP}$ $[_{VP}$ just arrived] $[_{CP}$ which I want to read]$_1$].

The relative clause modifying the head (i.e., *author*) of the subject DP can be extraposed as in (14a), whereas the one modifying the head (i.e., *article*) of the more deeply embedded DP cannot as in (14b). The extraposition in (14b) crosses two DPs, thus violating the Subjacency Condition.

As stated in (13), IP constitutes a bounding node for English.

(15) a. $[_{IP}$ $[_{CP}$ That $[_{IP}$ $[_{DP}$ a man t_1] $[_{VP}$ $[_{VP}$ is coming to dinner] $[_{CP}$ who I want to meet$]_1$]]] $[_{VP}$ is unusual]].

b. *$[_{IP}$ $[_{CP}$ That $[_{IP}$ $[_{DP}$ a man t_1] $[_{VP}$ is coming to dinner]]] $[_{VP}$ $[_{VP}$ is unusual] $[_{CP}$ who I want to meet$]_1$]]. *RRC

In (15a) the extraposition happens out of DP within IP. (15b), a case of the RRC violation, is subsumed by Subjacency because the extraposition crosses both DP and IP at once.

The Subjacency Condition accounts for a CNPC violation. The examples in (16) would have the SS representations in (17).

(16) a. Who does Steve believe Kono claimed that Ted admires?

b. *Who does Steve believe [the claim that Ted admires]? *CNPC

(17) a. $[_{CP}$ who_1 does $[_{IP}$ Steve believe $[_{CP}$ t''_1 $[_{IP}$ Kono claimed $[_{CP}$ t'_1 that $[_{IP}$ Ted admires t_1]]]]]]

b. *$[_{CP}$ who_1 does $[_{IP}$ Steve believe $[_{DP}$ the claim $[_{CP}$ t'_1 that $[_{IP}$ Ted admires t_1]]]]]

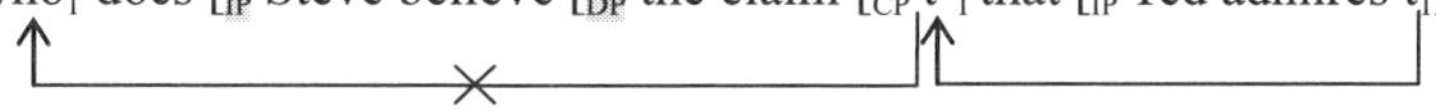

In (17a) each link of the chain formulated by the long-distance wh-movement satisfies Subjacency. In (17b), however, the link of [who_1, t'_1] violates Subjacency because it is created by crossing over two bounding nodes, DP and IP.

To summarize, it seems that the Subjacency Condition captures several bounding phenomena such as the Wh-island Constraint as in (11b), Superraising as in (12b), the RRC as in (15b), the CNPC as in (16b), and the AC as in (21). However, it does not capture the effects of the SSC as in (19) and the SC as in (20b).

6.4 Barriers

The notion of **barriers** is proposed to unify locality restrictions on **movement** and **government.**

(18) Government (*Barriers* version)
α governs β if
a. α is a governor,
b. α m-commands β, and
c. there is no barrier between α and β.

The following violates Ross's (1967) SSC, which cannot be subsumed by Subjacency. It observes Subjacency, as shown below, but is not grammatical.

√SUBJACENCY (19) *[$_{CP}$ Who$_1$ was$_2$ [$_{IP}$ [$_{CP}$ t_1 that [$_{IP}$ you met t_1]] t_2 unexpected]]?

In general, extraction is easier out of complement than subject domains. Hence, the grammatical (20a) causes a problem for Subjacency. Note that the shaded DP is the complement in (20a) and the subject in (20b).

*SUBJACENCY (20) a. [$_{CP}$ Who$_1$ did [$_{IP}$ you draw [$_{DP}$ a picture of t_1]]]?
*SUBJACENCY b. *[$_{CP}$ Who$_1$ did [$_{IP}$ [$_{DP}$ a picture of t_1] fall off the wall]]?

In addition, it is easier to extract something out of complement than adjunct domains. The following is ruled out by the Adjunct Condition (or the CED).

*SUBJACENCY (21) a. *[$_{CP}$ Who$_1$ did [$_{IP}$ he leave [$_{CP}$ because [$_{IP}$ he met t_1]]]]?
ADJUNCT CP
*SUBJACENCY b. *[$_{CP}$ When$_1$ did [$_{IP}$ he meet Kono [$_{DP}$ the day before t_1]]]?
ADJUNCT DP

If the wh-element moves directly to the matrix Spec of CP, the ungrammaticality of (21a) can be explained by Subjacency since the wh-movement moves across two bounding nodes, the embedded IP and the matrix IP.♣ Assuming that Spec of DP is not available for a successive-cyclic wh-movement, the ungrammaticality of (21b) can be explained by Subjacency, crossing over two bounding nodes, DP and IP.

Chomsky (*Barriers*) proposes a new approach to bounding phenomena. Under this proposal, a node becomes a barrier to movement, not because of its inherent character, but because of its residence in a structure. A potential barrier may avoid barrierhood due to an appropriate relation to a lexical head. What matters is now a **structure**.

A complement has a special feature of avoiding barrierhood. This special feature is called **L-marking**. Recall that a complement is related to a lexical head via **selection**. More precisely, a complement is L-marked, whereas a subject and an adjunct are not. The non-L-marked XP becomes a barrier to movement. There is one exception, IP, which is inherently not a barrier.

To solve this glitch, Chomsky defines barriers via the notion of blocking categories (BCs). The barrier defined in (23) is called **inherent barrier**.

(22) A movement which crosses a barrier is ungrammatical.

(23) a. An XP is a barrier if it is a BC but not IP.
b. An XP is a BC if it is not L-marked.
c. An XP is L-marked if it is selected by a lexical head.

CP inherits barrierhood from the IP which is a BC for an element that it contains. That is, a complement CP can become a barrier, even if it is L-marked, by dominating a BC for a moving element. An element within IP would thus be permitted to move out of that IP because this

♣ However, if the wh-element drops by the embedded Spec of CP, the ungrammaticality of (21a) cannot be ruled out by Subjacency.

is not a barrier but only a BC. However, this element could not move out of the CP in one giant leap. A consequence is then that only a movement to Spec of CP is legitimate.

In (24a) the IP is a BC. The CP is L-marked, but it can become an **inherited barrier**. In (24b) the CP is not a barrier for the wh-movement because *who* does not cross over the CP. In (24c) the CP is not a barrier for the wh-movement because it is not an inherited barrier this time.

(24) a. He thinks [$_{CP}$ [$_{IP}$ she likes who]]
BC BC
BA

b. He thinks [$_{CP}$ who$_1$ [$_{IP}$ she likes t$_1$]]

c. Who$_1$ does he think [$_{CP}$ t'$_1$ [$_{IP}$ she likes t$_1$]]?

6.5 Relativized Minimality

Like *Barriers*, Rizzi's (1990) Relativized Minimality approach does not set up absolute barrierhood to movement.

(25c) is an example of **Superraising**. An argument cannot cross over another argument.

EVIDENCE 1

(25) a. It$_1$ seems t$_1$ to be likely that Steve will win.

b. Steve$_1$ seems t$_1$ to be likely t$_1$ to win.

c. *Steve$_1$ seems that it is likely t$_1$ to win.

(26c) violates the **Wh-island Constraint**. A wh-element cannot cross over another wh-element.

EVIDENCE 2

(26) a. Who$_2$ t$_2$ wondered how$_1$ Steve fixed the car t$_1$?
b. How$_1$ did you say t$_1$ Steve fixed the car t$_1$?
c. *How$_2$ do you wonder who$_1$ t$_1$ fixed the car t$_2$?

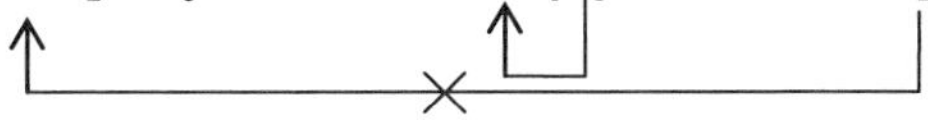

(27c) violates the Head Movement Constraint (**HMC**). A head cannot cross over another head.

EVIDENCE 3

(27) a. Could$_1$ they t$_1$ have left?
b. Have$_1$ they t$_1$ left?
c. *Have$_1$ they could t$_1$ left?

In this light, Rizzi (1990) proposes the Principle of Relativized Minimality, which reduces (operative) computational complexity.

(28) **Relativized Minimality**
No X can move over another X, where X is a head, an argument or a wh-element.

(29) X$_3$ X$_2$ X$_1$

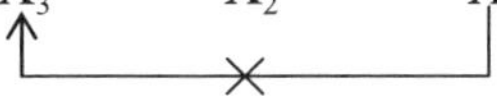

(Numbers on X for expository purposes only)

Exercise 6

《 6-1 》

Explain what the A-over-A Principle is. (Do not exceed the length of 10 lines.)

《 6-2 》

Discuss at least five types of island contraints, illustrating examples. (Do not exceed the length of 20 lines.)

《 6-3 》

Which island constraints can be explained by the Subjacency Condition? (Do not exceed the length of 20 lines.)

《 6-4 》

What is the main motivation of barriers? (Do not exceed the length of 20 lines.)

《 6-5 》

Discuss the three arguments for Relativized Minimality. (Do not exceed the length of 20 lines.)

7 Case Theory

Case Theory is a module of grammar that accounts for some properties of overt nominals, and integrates the notion of Case into Transformational Generative Grammar.

7.1 Abstract Case: Structural Case vs. Inherent Case

In GB, SS is motivated for Case reasons. DPs may have different phonetic shapes.

(1) $[_{IP}$ He$_{Nom}$ $[_{I'}$ will $[_{VP}$ t admire him$_{Acc}$]]].

Some structural positions license particular Cases.

(2)

	Position	Case	Example
a.	Subject of finite IP	Nominative Case	He left.
b.	Object of transitive V	Accusative Case	I saw him.
c.	Subject of DP	Genitive Case	his belief
d.	Complement of P	Accusative Case	near him

The **Case Filter**, a core part of Case Theory in GB, requires that every overt nominal receive **abstract** Case. This condition acts as a filter because it excludes any overt nominal phrase which is not assigned Case.

(3) The Case Filter (Chomsky *KL*: 74)
Every phonetically realized [DP] must be assigned (abstract) Case.

A-movement is motivated by Case. Movement of a DP from one Case position to another is prohibited in compliance with **Last Resort**. Example (4), a case of **Hyperraising**, shows the impossibility of A-movement out of finite clauses.

(4) *Steve$_1$ seems [t$_1$ knows the answer].

An A-position stands for an argument position. θ-roles are assigned to an A-position.

(5) [$_{IP}$ [$_{VP}$ Robin [$_{V}$ loves linguistics]]]
A-POS A-POS

An A-bar (A') position stands for a non-argument position.♣

(6) What did you buy t?
A'-POS A-POS

In some languages, Case is morphologically realized, and in others not. We assume that it is assigned in a uniform way whether it is morphologically realized or not.

(7) 철수가 영희를 보았다.
Chelswu-ka Yenghuy-lul po-ass-ta.
C-Nom Y-Acc see-Past-Dec
'Chelswu saw Yenghuy.'

There are two types of abstract Case: Structural Case and Inherent Case.

♣
Below, two different definitions of A-position vs. A'-position are provided:
(i) Chomsky (*LGB*: 45): An A-position is one in which an argument such as a name or a variable may appear in D-structure; it is a potential θ-position. The position of subject may or may not be a θ-position, depending on properties of the associated VP. Complements of X' are always θ-positions... An A'-position is that of an adjunct of one sort or another.
(ii) Chomsky and Lasnik (1995: 64): Given a lexical head L, we say that a position is L-related if it is the specifier or complement of a feature of L. The L-related positions are the former A-positions [i.e., the non-L-related positions are A'-positions]...

In Chomsky (*LGB*), A- and A'-positions are defined in terms of potential θ-positions, as shown in (i). As pointed out in Chomsky and Lasnik (1995), however, this definition is not straightforward in that a certain position needs to be regarded as an A-position despite the fact that there is no θ-relation to its head.

(iii) Spec of IP	Spec of VP
A-POS	A-POS
non-θ-POS	θ-POS

(8) a. **Structural Case**: Nominative Case is assigned to a subject DP by I in IP. Accusative Case is assigned to an object DP by V in VP or by P in PP.

b. **Inherent Case** is assigned to a DP by a lexical head that governs and assigns a θ-role to that DP.

The **Visibility Condition** states that a predicate can only assign a θ-role to a DP that is visible.

(9) The Visibility Condition (Chomsky *KL*)
A syntactic element must be Case-marked for it to be θ-marked.

+CASE → +θ

In order to be visible, a DP must be Case-marked with abstract Case.

(10) He hit the ball.

Depending on contexts, nonfinite clauses choose an overt lexical subject or a covert subject.

(11) a. $[_{CP}$ For $[_{IP}$ Steve to win]] would take a miracle.
b. *$[_{CP}$ $[_{IP}$ Steve to win]] would take a miracle.
c. $[_{CP}$ $[_{IP}$ PRO to win]] would take a miracle.

(12) a. Steve was happy $[_{CP}$ for $[_{IP}$ Danny to win]].
b. *Steve was happy $[_{CP}$ $[_{IP}$ Danny to win]].
c. Steve was happy $[_{CP}$ $[_{IP}$ PRO to win]].

The contrast between (11a, 12a) and (11b, 12b) shows that an overt subject in infinitive clauses requires the complementizer *for*. When the complementizer is absent, only the null subject PRO is allowed as in (11c) and (12c). It is assumed that the complementizer *for* behaves like a semantically null preposition, assigning accusative Case. (11b) and (12b) are ruled out by the Case Filter since the lexical subject of the infinitival clause is not Case-marked.

7.2 Case under Government

Vs and Ps can assign accusative Case to their complements, respectively.

(13) a. I love him.
b. I sent a letter to her.

Finite INFLs can assign nominative Case to their subjects.

(14) a. He might like Kono.
b. She is loved by Steve.

The overt subject in nonfinite clauses receives accusative Case. Case is not always assigned by a thematic element. In (15a) the complementizer *for* is the Case assigner. In (15b) the matrix verb is the Case assigner. Note that in (15b) *believes* assigns a θ-role to the embedded clause itself, not just to the subject of the embedded clause.

(15) a. For {him, *he} to leave now would be unacceptable.
b. I believe {her, *she} to be rich.

There are three configurations of Case assignment.

(16) a. from a V or P to its complement
b. from a finite inflection to its specifier
c. from a complementizer to the specifier of its IP complement (setting aside ECM)

(17) a. Acc

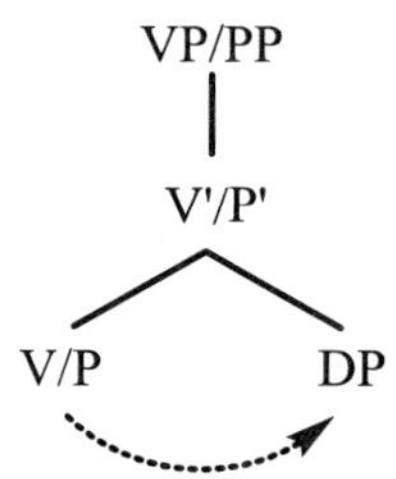

b. Nom

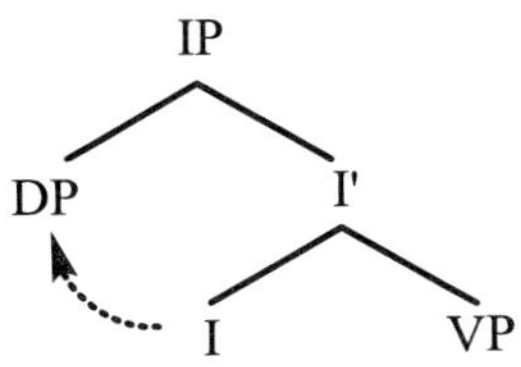

c. Acc

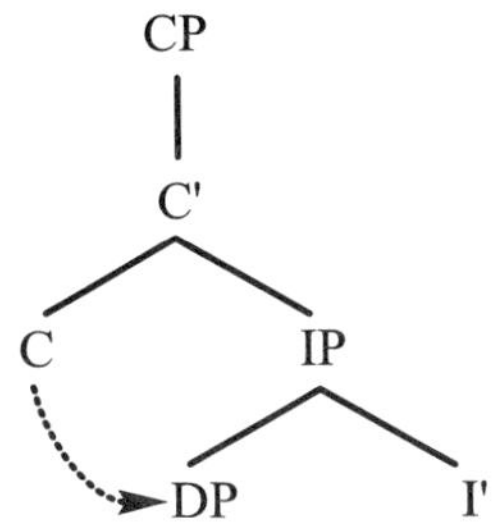

Case is assigned under government. Heads are not always governors.

(18) α is a **governor** if α = X^0 (not nonfinite INFL).

You can change the linear order of two complement PPs.

(19) a. I spoke [to the students] [about the assignment].
b. I spoke [about the assignment] [to the students].

But you cannot change the linear order of a DP complement and a PP complement.

(20) a. He put [the book] [on the shelf].
b. *He put [on the shelf] [the book].

There is an **adjacency** requirement with respect to licensing accusative Case.

(21) a. *We were anxious for tomorrow him to arrive early.
b. *I believe sincerely him to be rich.

But there is no adjacency requirement with respect to licensing nominative Case.

(22) He obviously will correct the error.

Given the Head-Complement configuration, Vs and Ps assign accusative Case to their sister DPs.

(23) a. $[_{VP}$ V $DP_{Acc}]$

b. $[_{PP}$ P $DP_{Acc}]$

Given the Spec-Head configuration, finite INFLs assign nominative Case to their Spec, and the possessive determiner *'s* genitive Case.

(24) a. $[_{IP}$ He_{Nom} $[_{I'}$ I_{FIN} VP]]

b. $[_{DP}$ $Steve_{Gen}$ $[_{D'}$'s NP]]

In short, it seems that Case licensing requires two distinct structural configurations: **Head-Complement** and **Spec-Head**.

These Case licensing configurations may be unified under the notion of **Case government**.

(25) α Case-marks β if and only if α governs β.

(26) α governs β if and only if α and β m-command each other.

(27) α m-commands β if and only if

a. α and β do not dominate each other, and

b. every maximal projection dominating α also dominates β, and

c. α does not equal β.

But there is a problem. In the following, each pronoun occupies the Spec of an infinitival IP, where α (i.e., *expects* or *for*) does not govern β (i.e., *him*) because of the **mutual** m-command requirement between α and β.

(28) a. Steve $[_{VP}$ expects $[_{IP}$ her to win]].

b. $[_{CP}$ For $[_{IP}$ him to leave]] would be terrible.

(29)

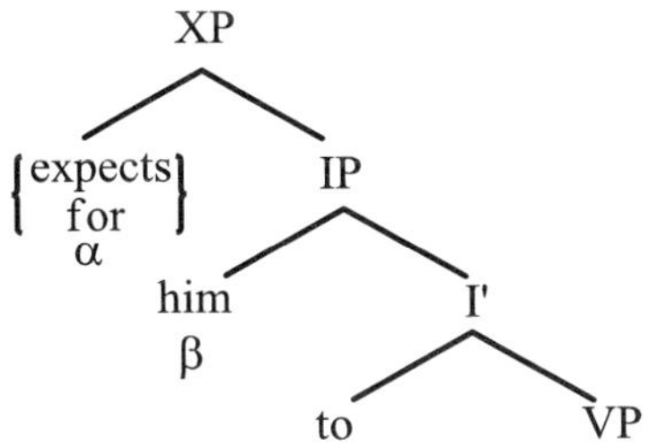

The following violates the Case Filter. The shaded pronouns are not Case-marked.

(30) a. *It was $[_{VP}$ expected $[_{IP}$ her to win]].

b. *$[_{CP}$ Him to leave] would be terrible.

There seems to be a way out. Let's revise the definition of **government** in terms of **barriers**. Given (31) and (32), *expects* and *for* in (28) govern and assign Case to the pronoun in Spec of IP. The IP is a complement so that it is not a barrier.

(31) α governs β if and only if CF. (26)

a. α m-commands β, and

b. there is no barrier γ that dominates β but does not dominate α.

(32) γ is a barrier if and only if

a. γ is a maximal projection, and

b. γ is not a complement.

7.3 Case and A-movement

7.3.1 Raising

At SS, the subject of a lower clause may be realized as the subject of a higher clause as in (33). This type of movement is possible with **raising verbs**.

(33) Steve$_1$ seems [t$_1$ to have traveled around the world].

In the following, the movement of *Steve* is obligatory due to the Case Filter.

(34) a. *Seems Steve to know the answer.
b. *It seems Steve to know the answer.

In compliance with Last Resort, raising is triggered by Case. In (35b) *Steve* should stay in its own clause because its Case requirement is satisfied in the embedded clause.

(35) a. Steve$_1$ seems [t$_1$ to like Kono].
b. It seems [Steve likes Kono].

The subject moves from Spec of VP to Spec of IP under the Predicate-Internal Subject Hypothesis (PISH). In Spec of IP, it receives Case and satisfies the EPP.

(36) [$_{IP}$ He$_1$ will [$_{VP}$ t$_1$ write a letter]].

7.3.2 Passivization

Passive Vs lack the ability to license Case on a complement. That is why (37c) and (37d) are ungrammatical, violating the Case Filter. (37c) also violates the EPP.

(37) a. This problem was solved.
+CASE

b. ____ was solved this problem — DS

c. *Was solved this problem. — *CASE FILTER, *EPP
-CASE

d. *It was solved this problem. — *CASE FILTER, √EPP
+CASE -CASE

Which element causes the ungrammaticality of (38b)? *Steve* violates the Case Filter. In (38c) *of* is a semantically null preposition.

(38) a. I [$_{VP}$ suspect Steve].

b. *I am [$_{AP}$ suspicious Steve].

c. I am suspicious of Steve.

The *of*-insertion strategy is not available for passive Vs.

(39) *It was solved of the problem

In short, we conclude that passive Vs are neither fully Vs nor fully As.

Nouns do not license Case on their complements.

(40) a. *[$_{DP}$ Lily's proof the theorem]

b. Lily [$_{VP}$ proved the theorem].

Nouns allow *of*-insertion.

(41) Lily's proof of the theorem

Movement into a subject position is often allowed. The structure of (42) is given in (43a) under a DP analysis of nominals and the UTAH. Compare (43a) with (43b), which shows an NP analysis of nominals.

(42) the theorem's proof

(43) a. DP analysis

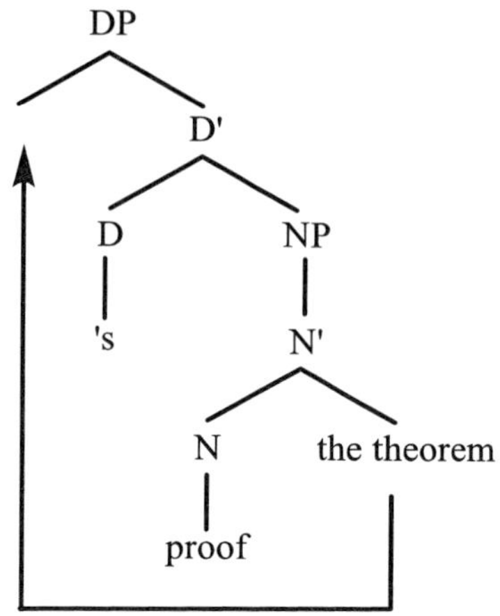

b. NP analysis

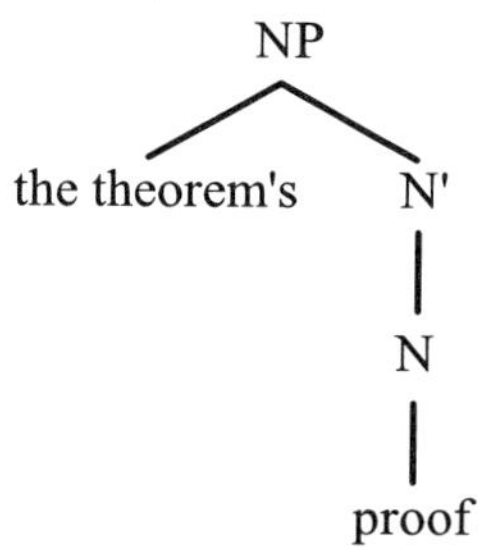

There are four major lexical categories: V, P, N, and A.

Regarding the licensing of Case on a complement, Vs and Ps pattern together. Regarding the triggering of the *of*-insertion strategy, Ns and As pattern together.

In this light, it is assumed that lexical categories are composed of binary distinctive features.

(44) a. V [+v, -n]
b. N [-v, +n]

c. A [+v, +n]
d. P [-v, -n]

What category can assign Case?

(45) Vs and Ps [-n]

Which category permits *of*-insertion?

(46) As and Ns [+n]

In Chomsky (*LGB*), Ns and As are not Case assigners.

(47) a. *a picture Chin Ho
b. *very fond his mother

Chomsky (*KL*) proposes that Ns and As assign **inherent Case** to their complements. Inherent Case is realized with the insertion of expletive *of*. Under this proposal, **Case licensing** consists of two parts. **Case assignment** and **Case realization**.

(48) a. a picture of Chin Ho
b. very fond of his mother

Of-insertion does not salvage (49) because only [+n] elements allow *of*-insertion.

(49) *of [Steve to leave now would be rude]

Passive Vs are similar to As.

(50) a. Steve was interrogated. vs. Steve was tall.
b. the interrogated man vs. the tall man

However, passive Vs do not license genitive Case. They do not tolerate *of*-insertion. We assume that passive Vs are specified just as [+v].

(51) *It was interrogated of Steve.

In the following, the active V *reported* assigns Case across an IP boundary as in (52):

ECM (52) They reported [$_{IP}$ the situation to be getting worse].
+CASE

However, the passive V *reported* cannot assign Case across an IP boundary as in (53). (53a) violates the Case Filter. Note that this is a special property of passive Vs. In (53b) the infinitival embedded subject moves from a Caseless position in DS to a Case-marked position in SS. The obligatory character of this movement also follows from the Case Filter.

(53) a. *It was reported [$_{IP}$ the situation to be getting worse].
-CASE

b. The situation$_1$ was reported [$_{IP}$ t_1 to be getting worse].
+CASE -CASE

In this light, Jaeggli (1986) proposes that passivization does not take place in the Lexicon and is syntactic in nature. The external θ-role and the Case of a V are assigned to the passive morpheme *-en* itself.

7.3.3 Unaccusative and Middle Constructions

According to **Burzio's** (1986) **Generalization**, Vs without an Agent argument also lack the ability to assign Case to their complements.

(54)

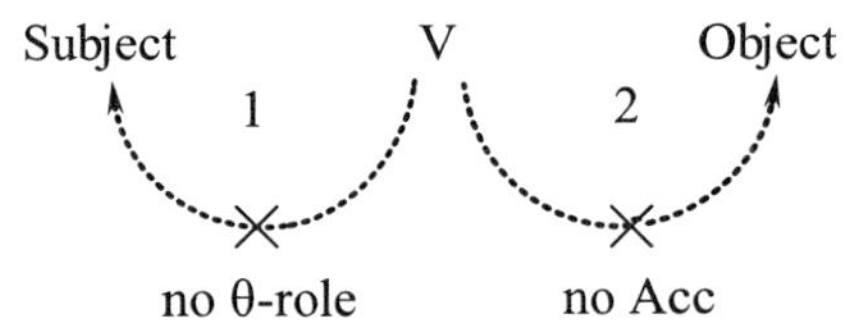

Some object obligatorily moves to a subject position. Verbs such as *arrive* or *break* are called **unaccusative** (= **ergative**) Vs.♣

(55) a. Three men_1 arrived t_1.
b. *It_{expl} arrived three men.

(56) a. The $base_1$ broke t_1.
b. *It_{expl} broke the base.

The **middle** voice is in the middle of the active and the passive voice because it is syntactically active but semantically passive. Verbs such as *mash*, *sell*, or *scare* are called middle Vs. Note that middle Vs strongly require an adverbial or negation.

(57) a. These $potatoes_1$ mash t_1 *(well).
b. The $book_1$ did *(not) sell t_1.
c. The bank $manager_1$ scared t_1 *(easily).

7.3.4 Exceptional Case-Marking (ECM)

Exceptional Case-Marking (ECM) verbs assign accusative Case to the subject of an infinitival embedded clause. The verb *believe* in (58) is the only Case assigner available. It is assumed that the embedded clause does not project CP. Since IP is not a barrier to government, *believe* governs *him* and assigns accusative Case to *him*.

(58) I believe [$_{IP}$ him to be rich].

The following is ruled out since ECM verbs do not select CP complements.

(59) *I believe [$_{CP}$ for him to be rich].

When CP is projected, it becomes a barrier to Case assignment from a higher clause.

(60) *He_1 doesn't know [$_{CP}$ whether [$_{IP}$ him_1 to go on vacation tomorrow]].
BA

♣ (55b) and (56b) violate the Case Filter in that the object (= internal argument) is Caseless.

PRO is the only legitimate subject in a nonfinite clause with CP.

(61) He$_1$ doesn't know [$_{CP}$ whether [$_{IP}$ **PRO**$_1$ to go on vacation tomorrow]].
BA

Considering the **Subjacency** Condition, however, (62) constitutes some evidence that the infinitival complement of *believe* must project CP at some point of derivation.

(62) [$_{CP}$ Who$_1$ does [$_{IP}$ Steve believe [$_{CP}$ t'$_1$ [$_{IP}$ t$_1$ to be the culprit]]]]?

Hence, we might presumably have to assume a rule called **CP-deletion** which deletes the CP boundary before Case is assigned.

Case and **θ-role** are related. According to the **Visibility Condition** in (9), a syntactic element (or a chain) must have Case at LF in order to be visible for θ-marking. Note that each example in (63) involves null operator (Op) movement. In (63a) the trace is ECMed by a higher V, while in (63b) it is not because the passivized *believed* lost the Case-licensing ability. In sum, (63b) violates the Visibility Condition.

(63) a. I met the man [Op$_1$ that Kono **believed** t$_1$ to be a genius].
+CASE

b. *I met the man [Op$_1$ that it **was believed** t$_1$ to be a genius].
-CASE

Exercise 7

《7-1》

Discuss the difference between Structural Case and Inherent Case. (Do not exceed the length of 10 lines.)

《7-2》

Discuss the different configurations of Case assignment. (Do not exceed the length of 10 lines.)

《7-3》

Explain what Case government is. (Do not exceed the length of 10 lines.)

《7-4》

Discuss the difference between Case assignment and Case realization. (Do not exceed the length of 10 lines.)

《7-5》

Discuss the configuration of Exceptional Case-Marking. Why is it exceptional? Provide a relevant example and its tree structure. (Do not exceed the length of 20 lines.)

《7-6》

Explain what the Visibility Condition is. (Do not exceed the length of 10 lines.)

Norbert Hornstein

http://ling.umd.edu/~hornstein/

- Expertise: Syntactic Theory, Linguistic Evolution, Logical Form, etc.
- Institutions: University of Maryland (since 1983), Columbia University (1979-1983), Harvard University (1978-1979)
- Degrees: Harvard University (PhD), McGill University (BA)
- Known for: Adjunction, Control, Labeling, Logical Form, Sideward Movement, etc.

8 Logical Form

In *The Little Prince* (French: *Le Petit Prince*), Antoine de Saint-Exupéry says:

(1) Voici mon secret. Il est très simple: on ne voit bien qu'avec le cœur. L'essentiel est invisible pour les yeux.
'Here is my secret. It is very simple: It is only with the heart that one can see rightly; what is essential is invisible to the eye.'

What you see is not what you get. This reflects an aspect of Logical Form (LF).

More linguistically, if there is an overt process in language A, and language B doesn't show that overt process, the process might still happen in language B covertly. That is, every language may be uniform in the covert component called LF.

This chapter aims to explore the issue of why Grammar needs LF.

8.1 Frege's Puzzle

According to logician Frege, **concepts** and **objects** are distinct. In the mathematical statement in (2a), parentheses correspond to concepts, and integers to objects.

(2)	a.	proposition:	(3) + (4) = (7)
	b.	concept:	( ) + ( ) = ( )
	c.	object:	3, 4, 7, etc.

In the following sentence, a predicate like *love* corresponds to a concept with argument slots. The two slots of dyadic *love* are filled with arguments: *Steve* and *Catherine*. The arguments are objects in the sense of Frege. Note that the objects in (3) are not scope-taking terms.

(3) Steve loves Catherine.

Frege observes the difference between **names** as in (3) and **quantifiers** as in (4). In (4) the quantifier *everyone* is not an object but a scope-taking term.

(4) Steve loves everyone.
'For anyone who exists, that person is loved by Steve.'

What is interesting is that a quantifier acts as a normal DP in other occasions.

(5) a. Steve loves [{everyone, a certain woman} and his dog].
b. {Everyone, A certain woman} is loved by Steve.
c. {Everyone, A certain woman} Steve loves is in the party.

A quantifier can be coordinated with a typical DP as in (5a). It can be the subject of a passive construction as in (5b). It can be the antecedent of a relative clause as in (5c).

A predicate such as V or A does not exhibit these properties.

The duality of a **quantifier**, a **semantic concept** as in (4) and a **syntactic object** as in (5), is called **Frege's puzzle**. This puzzle motivates linguists to postulate the abstract LF level of representations.

8.2 Quantifier Raising

In the tradition of Generative Grammar, linguists have believed that quantifiers like *everyone* or *someone* are concepts rather than objects. Especially, May (1977, 1985) uses LF to provide the appropriate representations for quantifiers.

Scope refers to the **semantic influence** of a given element, defined as follows:

(6) Scope Principle
α has scope over β if and only if α c-commands β.

With this in mind, consider again the following:

(7) a. [$_{VP}$ Steve loves everyone] DS
b. [$_{IP}$ Steve$_1$ I [$_{VP}$ t$_1$ loves everyone]]. SS

Everyone doesn't c-command the VP either at DS and SS. Intuitively speaking, however, (7) suggests that *everyone* should take a higher scope, being interpreted as in (8).

(8) For every relevant person x, Steve loves x

In order to understand how quantifiers are interpreted in English, let's consider Hungarian. As Szabolcsi (1997) shows, Hungarian provides an interesting window into the interpretation of quantifiers.

(9)	a.	Janos	Marit	szereti.
		Janos-Nom	Mari-Acc	loves
		'Janos loves Mari.'		
	b.	MARIT/kit	Janos	szereti.
		Mari(FOC)/who-Acc	Janos-Nom	loves
		'It is Mari/who is it that Janos loves.'		
	c.	Mindenkit	Janos	szereti.
		Everyone-Acc	Janos-Nom	loves
		'Janos loves everyone.'		

It has been reported that focalization in Hungarian is overt and obligatory as in (9b). Of particular interest is that the **quantifier** in (9c) is **overtly** and **obligatorily** fronted to a scope-taking position, too.

Therefore, we have a good reason to mimic this process of movement for the interpretation of English quantifiers, as a way to solve Frege's puzzle.

Chomsky (1976) argues that operators move to a scope-taking position **covertly** as well as **overtly**.

(10) a. His$_1$ mother loves Steve$_1$.

OVERT MOVEMENT — b. *Who$_1$ does his$_1$ mother love t$_1$?

COVERT MOVEMENT — c. *His$_1$ mother loves STEVE$_1$.

In (10a) *his* can refer to *Steve*. But it can't refer to *who* in (10b). This is a so-called **Strong Crossover** effect (Postal 1971). What is interesting is that (10c) seems to reveal the same effect where *STEVE* is focalized. Let's assume that the focused phrase moves covertly to a scope-taking position. Then, we can rule out both (10b) and (10c) in the same way.

As predicted, the Strong Crossover effect is observed in sentences with Frege's puzzle.

COVERT MOVEMENT

(11) a. Everyone$_1$ loves his$_1$ mother.

b. *His$_1$ mother loves everyone$_1$.

In (11a) *his* refers to *everyone*, but not in (11b). If (11b) yields a Strong Crossover effect, and the Strong Crossover effect is addressed via an operator movement, then (11b) might contain a covert operator movement.

Let's consider the following example in (12), which shows **scope ambiguity**.

AMBIGUOUS

(12) Someone loves everyone.

(13) a. There exists a (very loving) x such that for every y, x loves y. ($\exists$ = WS)

b. For every y, there is (in this lucky world) some x or other who loves y. ($\forall$ = WS)

In (13a) the existential quantifier ($\exists$) *someone* takes the wide scope (WS), and in (13b) the universal quantifier ($\forall$) *everyone* does so.

May (1977) proposes a covert process of Quantifier Raising (**QR**) in order to account for the scopal properties in (12). In compliance with QR, every quantifier must take a scope-taking position at LF. If QR applies first to the universal quantifier and then to the existential quantifier, we derive the rigid scope reading as in (14), according to the Scope Principle. If QR applies first to the existential quantifier, and then to the universal quantifier, we derive the inverse scope reading as in (15). May (1977) simply assumes that QR is an S-adjunction (= IP-adjunction) operation.

RIGID SCOPE

(14) $[_{IP}$ someone$_2$ $[_{IP}$ everyone$_1$ $[_{IP}$ t$_2$ loves t$_1$]]]

INVERSE SCOPE

(15) $[_{IP}$ everyone$_2$ $[_{IP}$ someone$_1$ $[_{IP}$ t$_1$ loves t$_2$]]]

QR is unique. Unlike wh-movement, it is **clause-bounded**. In the following, the existential quantifier has always the wide scope reading.

UNAMBIGUOUS

(16) Someone believes [governments to cheat everyone].
WS NS

However, the following is ambiguous, which shows the scope interaction between the wh-phrase and the existential quantifier:

AMBIGUOUS

(17) Who$_1$ does someone believe [governments to cheat t$_1$]?

May (1985) changes the proposal in his dissertation (1977) to account for the contrast in (18).

AMBIGUOUS
UNAMBIGUOUS

(18) a. What did everyone buy for Max?
b. Who bought everything for Max?
WS NS

(18a) is scopally ambiguous. In the wide scope reading of the wh-phrase, everyone bought something particular for Max: WH = WS. In the wide scope reading of the universal quantifier, each individual had a (potentially different) buying relation: $\forall$ = WS.

(18b) is not ambiguous. It doesn't have a pair-list reading. The wh-phrase has always wide scope. There was somebody particular who bought everything for Max: WH = WS.

In order to rule out the pair-list reading in (18b), May (1985) adopts Pesetsky's (1982) **No Crossing-Path Condition** according to which the derivation involving crossing paths for the moved phrases is ill-formed. If QR is adjunction to IP, the derivation in (19a) for (18b) is ruled out by the No Crossing-Path Condition. The derivation in (19b) for (18b) is fine since the paths of movement phrases don't cross. Note that in May (1985) the QR from VP should be an adjunction to VP, not to IP, along with the No Crossing-Path Condition.

(19) a. *$[_{CP}$ who$_2$ $[_{IP}$ everything$_1$ $[_{IP}$ t$_2$ $[_{VP}$ buy t$_1$]]]] for Max *IP ADJUNCTION

b. $[_{CP}$ who$_1$ $[_{IP}$ t$_1$ $[_{VP}$ everything$_2$ $[_{VP}$ buy t$_2$]]]] for Max VP ADJUNCTION

What matters is then how the ambiguity in (18a) obtains. Since May (1985) doesn't assume the PISH, the universal quantifier originates in Spec of IP, and adjoins to IP in LF for the scope-taking process as in (20). Considering the validity of the No Crossing-Path Condition, it seems that we now have only one legitimate LF representation:

(20) $[_{CP}$ what$_2$ $[_{IP}$ everyone$_1$ $[_{IP}$ t$_1$ $[_{VP}$ buy t$_2$]]]] for Max

In order to address this issue, May (1985) revises the Scope Principle in (6) as follows:

(21) Scope Principle (May 1985)

Members of a **Σ-sequence** are free to take on any type of relative scope relation, where any two items A and B, are in a Σ-sequence if every maximal projection dominating A dominates B and vice versa, and A does not dominate B.

In (21) the scopal meaning is not read off directly at LF. That is, the ambiguity in (12) does not result from two different LFs.

In May (1985), the derivation in (14) is ill-formed due to the crossing path, and that in (15) is only well-formed. From the latter single derivation, May thus obtains two valid interpretations.

More concretely, according to the revised Scope Principle in (21), the two IP-adjoined quantifiers in (15) constitute a Σ-sequence, thus exchanging scope over each other.

√Σ-SEQUENCE

(22) for (15)

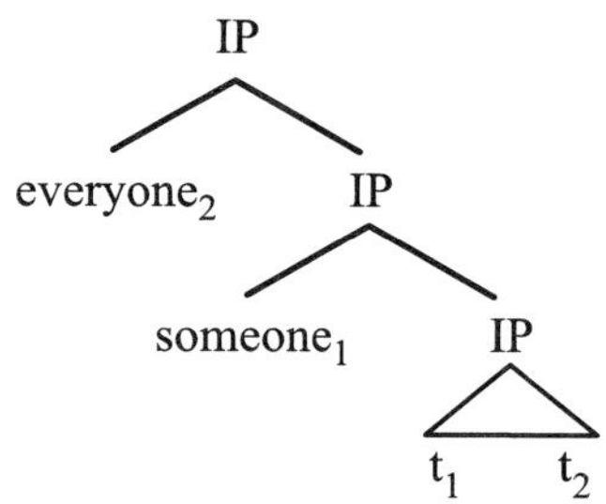

Returning to the ambiguity of (20), May argues that *what* and *everyone* form a Σ-sequence in that the segmented IPs created by adjunction do not fully dominate *everyone*, as shown below:

√Σ-SEQUENCE

(23) for (20)

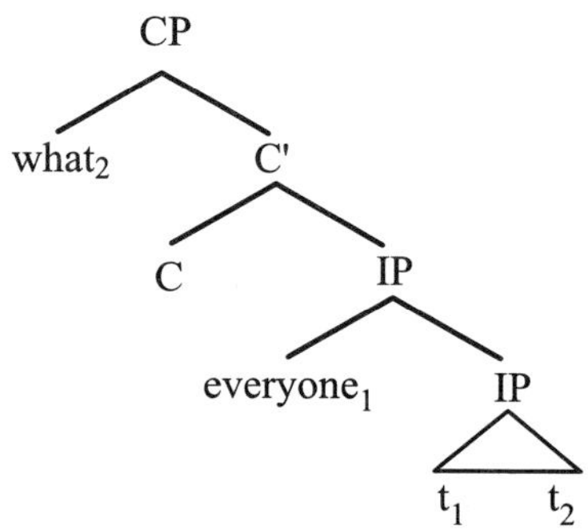

Regarding the unambiguous (19b), however, *who* and *everything* do not form a Σ-sequence, since the IP dominates *everything*, but excludes *who*, as shown below:

*Σ-SEQUENCE

(24) for (19b)

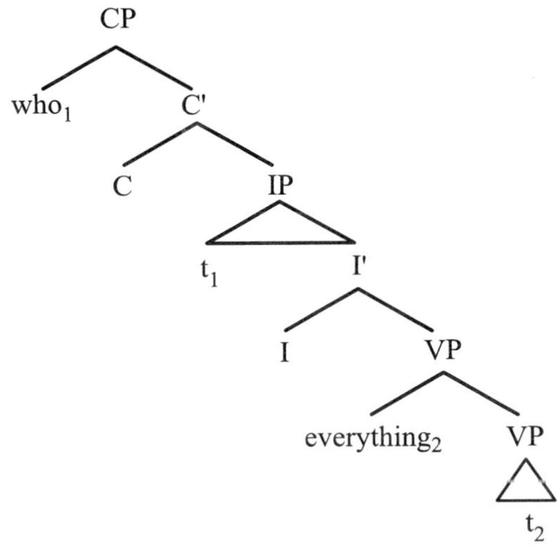

In short, QR is evidence of LF.

8.3 Wh-in situ

In languages like Chinese, wh-questions do not require overt wh-fronting, as shown below:

(25) Zhangsan xiang-zhidao Lisi mai-le sheme.
Zhangsan wonder Lisi bought what
'Zhangsan wonders what Lisi bought.'

But Huang (1982) argues that although there is no apparent wh-fronting, there might be covert wh-fronting in Chinese. He shows that covert wh-fronting in Chinese observes syntactic conditions. For example, he observes that (26) is ungrammatical in Chinese, just like what happens in English as in (27), violating the CNPC.

(26) *[Ni xiangxin [$_{island}$ [Lisi weisheme likai]
you believe Lisi why leave
de shuofa]]?
DE claim
'Why do you believe the claim that Lisi left?'

(27) *Why do [you believe [$_{island}$ the claim [t that [Lisi left t]]]]?

Huang's account is straightforward: the LFs of (26) and (27) are identical.

Huang (1982) provides additional argument for the covert wh-fronting of in-situ wh-phrases. In (28) some wh-fronting out of the complex nominal clause in Chinese is legitimate.

(28) Ta xiang-zhidao [ni xiangxin [[Lisi mai-le sheme]
he wonders you believe Lisi bought-Aspect what
de shuofa]]
DE claim
'He wonders what you believe the claim that Lisi bought.'

In order to put the following discussion into perspective, let's briefly discuss the notion of **Chain Uniformity**.

With respect to the displacement effects in natural language, Chomsky and Lasnik (1995) propose that all chains created by overt or covert movement must be uniform at LF. In fact, the inventory of movement up to LF would be as follows:

(29)	a.	(X^0,	X^0,	…,	X^0)	head movement
	b.	(A,	A,	…,	A)	A-movement
	c.	(A',	…,	A',	A)	A'-movement of an argument
	d.	(A',	A',	…,	A')	adjunct movement

(29a) shows a head movement chain, and (29b) an A-movement chain. (29c) shows an A'-movement chain of an argument, and (29d) an A'-movement chain of an adjunct. All of these chains are uniform except (29c). In order to make (29c) uniform, all intermediate traces would have to delete at LF, yielding the chain of (A', A). This is called an **operator-variable chain**. The legitimate chains at LF are then as follows:

(30)					
	a.	(X^0,	X^0,	…,	X^0)
	b.	(A,	A,	…,	A)
	c.	(A',	…,		A)
	d.	(A',	A',	…,	A')

Notice that A'-movement of arguments and that of adjuncts form two different kinds of chains at LF. Since **non-uniform chains** are **not legitimate LF objects**, **Last Resort** triggers deletion of the ill-formed links of chains for the benefit of **convergence**.

Returning to (28), Last Resort can delete the intermediate **offending trace** in order to form a uniform chain. The chain of the argument *sheme* in (31a) is not uniform. The result is the convergent chain in (31b).

(31) a. $sheme_1$ [ni xiangxin [t'_1 [Lisi mai-le t_1] de shuofa]]
*A'-TRACE A-TRACE

b. $sheme_1$ [ni xiangxin [[Lisi mai-le t_1] de shuofa]]

In short, the interpretation of wh-in situ happens at LF.

8.4 Antecedent-Contained Deletion

One argument for QR comes from the ellipsis of Antecedent-contained Deletion (ACD).

(32) Steve loves everyone that Danny does.

Bouton (1970) observes that (32) induces **self-referentiality**.

(33)

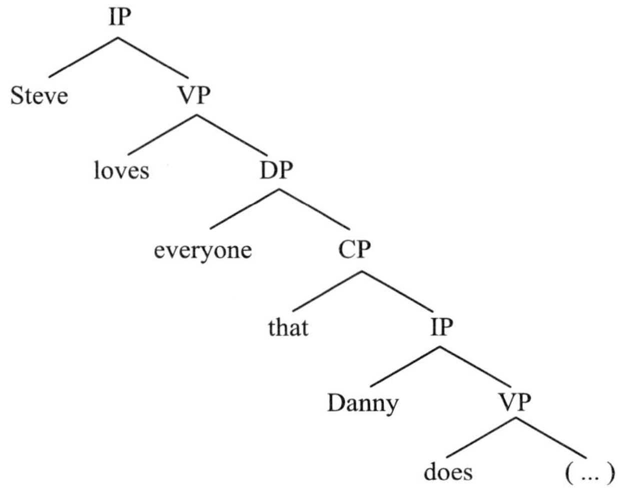

Suppose that **ellipsis** resolution is made via LF copying of a relevant antecedent in (either linguistic or pragmatic) discourse into the ellipsis site. The following shows an illustration:

(34) a. Steve loves his mother, and Danny does too.

LF b. Steve -s [$_{VP}$ love his mother], and Danny does [$_{VP}$ love his mother] too

A question is what the antecedent is in (33) for the purpose of LF copying. If the antecedent were the higher VP of [$_{VP}$ *loves everything that Danny does*], the LF copying process would have included the ellipsis site itself, inducing the problem of infinite regress.

In order to solve Bouton's puzzle, let's call upon QR in (32), fronting the quantifier phrase (QP) out of the VP site and adjoining to a higher position.

QR (35) [[everyone that Danny does ∅]$_1$ [Steve loves t$_1$]]

The ultimate landing site of the QP in (35) is not important insofar as it is **outside the VP**. The VP at issue is now something like [*loves t*], which can antecede the elliptic VP under identity without causing the issue of self-referentiality.

RECONSTRUCT

(36) [[everyone that Danny does ∅] [Steve loves t]]

In this way of ellipsis resolution, the QP involving the ACD should take scope over the antecedent VP.

EVIDENCE AGAINST QR

Baltin (1987) observes, however, that the QR approach to ACD is problematic in the case of multiple questions as follows:

(37) Who thought that Jack faced how many problems that Jill did?

Given the overt wh-movement and the subsequent covert QR, (37) would yield the LF in (38).

(38) [how many problems that Jill did]$_2$ who$_1$ [t$_1$ thought that Jack faced t$_2$]

If this is so, two ellipsis resolutions (i.e., the lower VP reading and the higher VP reading) should be available, as given below:

(39) a. [how many problems that Jill did]$_2$ who$_1$ [t$_1$ thought that Jack faced t$_2$]

b. *[how many problems that Jill did]$_2$ who$_1$ [t$_1$ thought that Jack faced t$_2$]

Baltin observes that the higher VP reading in (39b) is somehow unavailable by many speakers. It amounts to saying that **ACD** has a sort of **clause-boundedness**.

Given this spirit, Baltin argues that the prior movement in ACD is **extraposition** in that there is nothing special about the property of moving elements whether they are quantifiers or wh-phrases.

Extraposition is a **stylistic** rule according to which a heavy element prefers to appear in the right periphery of a clause. (40b) thus sounds better than (40a).

(40) a. I saw a man who wants to win the lottery tomorrow today.

b. I saw a man t_1 today who wants to win the lottery tomorrow$_1$.

With that in mind, consider the following:

(41) Steve [$_{VP}$ loves everyone t_1] these days who Danny does$_1$.

The relative clause in (41) undergoes extraposition to the right of *these days*. This process provides a way of ACD resolution. After the extraposition, the relative clause involving the ACD is safely outside the antecedent VP. Now, the antecedent VP can be copied to the ellipsis VP inside the extraposed relative clause at LF, thus getting out of the infinite regress dilemma.

The structural effect of extraposition seems to be the same as that of QR or wh-movement at LF. Furthermore, extraposition is **clause-bounded**. For example, (42a) becomes ill-formed if the relative clause is extraposed over an matrix adverbial (i.e., *until a year ago*) as in (42b).

(42) a. I believed [that Steve loves everyone that Danny loves] until a year ago.

b. *I believed [that Steve loves everyone t_1] until a year ago that Danny loves$_1$.

Ross (1967) rules out (42b) via the Right Roof Constraint (**RRC**) according to which rightward movement is limited to its own clause.

For Baltin, the unavailability of (39b) naturally follows in that the long-distance extraposition for a relevant ACD reading is banned by the RRC. If

Baltin is right on the track, one important argument for QR would collapse.

LOWER VP ADJUNCTION

HIGHER VP ADJUNCTION

(43) a. who thought [$_{CP}$ that Jack [$_{VP}$ faced t$_1$] [how many problems that Jill did]$_1$]

b. *who [$_{VP}$ thought [$_{CP}$ that Jack [$_{VP}$ faced t$_1$]] [how many problems that Jill did]$_1$]

EVIDENCE AGAINST EXTRAPOSITION

Larson and May (1990) observe that ACD is permitted when it is impossible to extrapose a relative clause. As in (44b) extraposition of the relative clause introduced by a **null complementizer** is not possible, but ACD is fine as in (44a).

(44) a. He put [every coat $\varnothing_C$ he could] on his broad shoulders.

b. *He put [every coat] on his broad shoulders $\varnothing_C$ he could.

In this light, they argue against Baltin's extraposition analysis of ACD.

PERPLEXING PUZZLE

May (1985) regards the following contrast as evidence of his QR approach to ACD:

(45) a. Dulles suspected everyone Angleton did.

b. *Dulles suspected Philby, who Angleton did.

In (45b) the shaded expression headed by the name *Philby* cannot undergo QR because it is not a QP. This contrast could be a challenge for Baltin's extraposition analysis. Extraposition is not likely to be sensitive to the quantificational properties of given nominals.

What is fairly puzzling is the grammaticality of (46). The acceptability of (45b) is significantly improved by discourse controllers like *not* or *as well*, as noted by Wyngaerd and Zwart (1991).

(46) a. Dulles suspected Philby, who Angleton did not.

b. Dulles suspected Philby, who Angleton did as well.

Apparently, QR is not responsible for this difference.

8.5 Reconstruction

Another piece of evidence for a syntactically active covert component results from the so-called *reconstruction*. Let's briefly consider why LF reconstruction process is motivated.

When wh-arguments move overtly into Spec of CP in order to form a wh-question, they leave behind wh-traces in original positions. That is, quantificational operators occupy Spec of CP, and variables original positions.

Given this, consider the following wh-questions:

(47) a. Whose mother did you see?
b. To who(m) did you talk?

An exemplary answer is given below, respectively, to each question in (47).

(48) a. I saw Danny's mother and Frank's mother.
b. I talked to Danny, and I talked to Frank.

The LFs of (48) are given below:

(49) a. who x you saw x's mother
b. who x you talked to x

Let's assume that speakers provide the following answers to the questions in (47). The answers in (50) might be acceptable, but are slightly off the mark.

(50) a. I saw Kono.
b. I talked about Ted.

To overcome this problem of potential difference between SS and LF, overtly moved wh-phrases can undergo **reconstruction** to their trace positions and then **raising** of just the wh-operator parts in LF.

(51) a. $[_{CP}$ whose mother$_1$ did $[_{IP}$ you see $t_1]]$ SS
b. $[_{CP}$ whose$_1$ did $[_{IP}$ you see $[t_1$ mother$]]]$ LF

(52) a. $[_{CP}$ to who(m)$_1$ did $[_{IP}$ you talk $t_1]]$ SS
b. $[_{CP}$ who(m)$_1$ did $[_{IP}$ you talk [to $t_1]]]$ LF

With this in mind, consider the referential dependency in (53).

(53) a. Which picture of himself did Steve like? SS
b. Which picture of Steve did he like? SS

If the LFs of (53) were not much different from their SS representations, then the subjects in (53) would not c-command into the syntactically fronted wh-domains. Given this scenario, (53a) poses a violation of Principle A in that the anaphor *himself* inside the dislocated wh-object is not c-commanded by its antecedent *Steve*. Similarly, the R-expression *Steve* cannot refer to the subject *he* in (53b) due to Principle C.

These predictions are fulfilled if the following LFs obtain. For the expository purpose, copies are used with < > instead of traces at LF.

(54) a. which did Steve like <picture of himself> LF
b. which did he like <picture of Steve> LF

There are so many issues to be addressed surrounding reconstruction, but we will pass over further discussion to chapter 9.

Exercise 8

《8-1》
What is Frege's Puzzle? (Do not exceed the length of 10 lines.)

《8-2》
Compare May's (1977) account with May's (1985) account of quantifier interpretation. (Do not exceed the length of 20 lines.)

《8-3》
Discuss the notion of Chain Uniformity. (Do not exceed the length of 10 lines.)

《8-4》
Discuss Baltin's (1987) approach to ACD resolution. (Do not exceed the length of 20 lines.)

《8-5》
Discuss the reconstruction arguement for LF. (Do not exceed the length of 20 lines.)

9 Binding Theory

Binding Theory has three principles on the structural relations between nominals.

9.1 Referential Dependency

Binding Theory is concerned with three types of nominals as follows:

(1) a. **Anaphors**: himself, themselves, each other, one another, etc.
 b. **Pronominals**: he, it, his, one, them, him, etc.
 c. **R-expressions**: Adam, Kono, desk, book, etc.

Anaphors are DPs that should receive reference from other referential expressions (i.e., antecedents) in a sentence.

(2) a. Steve killed himself.
 b. Adam and Kono loved each other.

Pronominals are DPs that may (but need not) receive reference from other DPs in linguistic or situational discourse.

(3) Ross said that he played basketball.
'Ross said that Ross played basketball.'
'Ross said that Chandler played basketball.'

R-expressions express content. They are DPs that refer to entities in the world.

(4) Barack Obama, Steve, the woman in the blue suit, a teddy bear, purple shoes, etc.

Antecedents are DPs that give their meaning to anaphors or pronominals.

(5) Steve shaved himself.

Indexing is a way of representing the meaning of a DP. Each index represents a different reference.

(6) a. [Ross]$_i$ gave [Chandler]$_j$ [a basketball]$_k$.
b. [Joey]$_i$ said that [he]$_j$ played [basketball]$_k$ in [the dark]$_l$.
c. [Joey]$_i$ said that [he]$_i$ played [basketball]$_k$ in [the dark]$_l$.
d. [Monica]$_i$ bopped [herself]$_i$ on [the head]$_j$ with [a flashlight]$_k$.

Let's consider the concept of **co-indexing** and **co-reference**.

(7) a. Two DPs that have the same index are said to be co-indexed.
b. Two DPs that are co-indexed are said to co-refer (that is, refer to the same entity in the world).

(8) a. [Joey]$_i$ said that [he]$_i$ played [basketball]$_k$ in [the dark]$_l$.
b. [Joey]$_i$ said that [he]$_j$ played [basketball]$_k$ in [the dark]$_l$.

Reflexive pronouns and reciprocal pronouns are anaphors.

(9) a. *Himself is tall.
b. He is tall.

(10) a. *Each other met.
b. The boys$_2$ said the girls$_1$ know each other$_{1/*2}$.

Personal pronouns are pronominals.

(11) a. Chin Ho$_1$ thinks the girls like him$_1$.
b. He left.
c. Chin Ho$_1$ likes him$_{*1}$.

Names are R-expressions.

(12) Adam said he liked Kono.

Let's consider the role of indices.

(13) a. Syntax and semantics are independent systems, related only by the semantic component interpreting syntactic representations.
b. Reference is partially represented by the syntactic device of an index.
c. Indices are structural elements which are interpreted semantically.

(14) a. Steve$_1$ thinks Danny$_2$ admires him$_1$.
b. *Steve$_1$ thinks Danny$_2$ admires him$_2$.

9.2 Binding Principles

Anaphors **need** a local antecedent. Pronominals **may have** an antecedent outside a certain local domain. Referential expressions **must not have** an antecedent; they must be free everywhere. These referential properties are encapsulated in three Binding Principles.

(15) a. Principle A: An anaphor must be bound locally.
b. Principle B: A pronominal must be free locally.
c. Principle C: An R-expression must be free everywhere.

Bind and *c-command* are defined as follows:

(16) α **binds** β if and only if

a. α and β are co-indexed, and

b. α c-commands β.

(17) An element **c-commands** its sister and everything dominated by its sister.

Finite clauses are always local domains (**LD**s).

(18) *Steve$_1$ believes [$_{LD}$ himself$_1$ is discreet].

Some nonfinite clause is a local domain, too.

(19) *Adam$_1$ believes [$_{LD}$ Kono to like himself$_1$].

However, other nonfinite clause does not count as a local domain.

(20) [$_{LD}$ Steve$_1$ believes [himself$_1$ to be discreet]].

Local domain is formally defined as governing category.

(21) Governing Category (temporary)

β is a governing category for α if β is the smallest clause which contains α and the governor γ of α.

(22) [$_{\beta}$ ... γ α ...]

Then, (15) is revised as follows.

(23) a. Principle A: An anaphor must be bound within its governing category.

b. Principle B: A pronominal must be free within its governing category.

c. Principle C: An R-expression must be free everywhere.

Below, the DP is a governing category.

(24) *Danny$_1$ saw [$_{DP=GC}$ Steve's picture of himself$_1$].

Below, the DP is not a governing category.

(25) $[_{GC}$ Danny$_1$ saw $[_{DP}$ a picture of himself$_1$]].

The possessor of a DP acts as the subject of a sentence.

(26) a. $[_{DP}$ the enemy's destruction of the city]
b. $[_{IP}$ The enemy destroyed the city].

Given this, (21) is revised as follows:

(27) **Governing Category** (final)
β is a governing category for α if β is the smallest IP or DP with a subject which contains α and the governor γ of α.

(28) $[_{\beta = IP/DP}$ ... SU ... γ α ...]

Three types of nominals are relevant for all DPs whether they are overt or covert.

DP traces are covert anaphors in that they behave like (overt) anaphors as follows:

(29) a. Steve$_1$ likes himself$_1$.
b. *Adam$_1$ believes Kono likes himself$_1$.
c. Steve$_1$ believes himself$_1$ to be honest.
d. *Steve$_1$ believes himself$_1$ is honest.

(30) a. Steve$_1$ was hurt t_1.
b. *Adam$_1$ was believed Kono likes t_1.
c. Steve$_1$ was believed t_1 to be strong.
d. *Adam$_1$ was believed t_1 likes Kono.

The **wh-traces** in an **A-position** are R-expressions. They are called **variables**. (32b) violates Principle C; the variable (i.e., R-expression) cannot be bound by an A-element. This violation was called *Strong Crossover* (**SCO**).

(31) a. Who$_1$ did Steve think [$_{CP}$ t$_1$ [$_{IP}$ Kono liked **t**$_1$]]?
b. Who$_1$ did Steve think [$_{CP}$ t$_1$ [$_{IP}$ **t**$_1$ liked Kono]]?

(32) a. Who$_1$ [$_{IP}$ **t**$_1$ thinks [$_{IP}$ he$_1$ should win]]?

SCO b. *Who$_1$ does [$_{IP}$ he$_1$ think [$_{IP}$ **t**$_1$ should win]]?

The following summarizes the types of referential elements.

(33)	ANAPHOR	PRONOMINAL	R-EXPRESSION
OVERT	reflexive, reciprocal	personal pronoun	proper noun
COVERT	A-trace	pro	variable

Let's reconsider the types of referential elements in terms of features such as [±pronominal, ±anaphor].

(34)	+PRONOMINAL	-PRONOMINAL	
+ANAPHOR	___	reflexive, reciprocal	OVERT
	PRO	A-trace	COVERT
-ANAPHOR	personal pronoun	proper noun	OVERT
	pro	variable	COVERT

Korean permits null subjects in finite clauses. They are marked as pro. English does not permit pro.

(35) a. pro 떠났어.
pro Ttena-ss-e.
leave-Past-Dec
'(He) left.'

CF. He left. b. *pro Left.

English permits a PRO subject in nonfinite clauses. Since PRO is a **pronominal anaphor**, it is subject to both Principle A and Principle B of Binding Theory. It follows from Binding Theory that PRO lacks a governing category, thus being ungoverned (Chomsky 1982: 21).

Why doesn't an overt pronominal anaphor exist? It's because such an element would always be contradictory.

(36) A **covert pronominal anaphor** (i.e., PRO) must satisfy both Principle A and Principle B because it is anaphoric and pronominal simultaneously. This **contradiction** can be **avoided** if it does not have a governing category. It is not subject to the Case Filter because it is a covert DP.

(37) An **overt pronominal anaphor** must not be governed since it is subject to both Principle A and Principle B. But its overtness requires that it be governed, given the concept of Case government. This is an **unavoidable contradiction**.

Binding Theory applies at certain syntactic levels of representation. An issue is whether three Binding Principles should be grouped under the umbrella of Binding Theory. Another issue is whether one principle or another applies at a different level from the others. In what follows, we will explore these issues. The PISH is suppressed for the sake of exposition.

9.3 Principle A

It seems that anaphors can be licensed either **before** or **after** movement. In (38a) the anaphor is bound at DS. In (38b) the anaphor is bound at SS. An issue is thus raised whether Principle A applies at DS or SS or both.

(38) a. [Which picture of himself$_2$]$_1$ did Steve$_2$ display t$_1$? DS (OR LF) EVIDENCE

b. [The men]$_1$ seem to each other$_1$ [t$_1$ to be smart]. SS (OR LF) EVIDENCE

Principle A apparently seems to be a **derivational** (or anywhere) **condition**.

If reconstruction is possible at LF, however, DS evidence of anaphor licensing may reduce to LF evidence. More precisely, if only the **non-**

wh-part of the DP is reconstructed into its original position, (39) would be the LF of (38a). << >> indicates an LF reconstructed part.

LF EVIDENCE

(39) LF: [which] did Steve display <<picture of himself>>

In addition, if the SS in (38b) is not much different from its LF, Principle A may be regarded as an LF condition.

(40) LF: [the men]$_1$ seem to each other$_1$ [t$_1$ to be smart]

Consider the following in which the anaphor is not bound in its governing category:

(41) ***Steve**$_1$ wondered [which woman] liked [which pictures of **himself**$_1$].

(41) could be used as evidence that Principle A must apply at DS or SS, assuming that covert movement moves the whole wh-phrase.

DS OR SS EVIDENCE

(42) LF: √[$_{TP}$ **Steve**$_1$ wondered [$_{CP}$ [which pictures of **himself**$_1$]$_3$+[which woman]$_2$ [$_{IP}$ t$_2$ liked t$_3$]]]

As an alternative, however, if covert wh-movement targets only a wh-element, Principle A may be formulated as an LF condition.

LF EVIDENCE

(43) LF: *[$_{IP}$ **Steve**$_1$ wondered [$_{CP}$ which$_3$+[which woman]$_2$ [$_{IP}$ t$_2$ liked [t$_3$ pictures of **himself**$_1$]]]]

The following sentence is ambiguous; *himself* could be *Steve* or *Ted.*

(44) Steve$_1$ wondered which picture of himself$_{1/2}$ Ted$_2$ liked.

If the downstairs reading (the embedded subject *Ted* reading) is possible, Principle A must apply at DS, as shown in (45a). If the upstairs reading (the matrix subject *Steve* reading) is possible, Principle A must apply at SS or LF, as shown in (45b). Again, Principles A looks like a derivational condition. It can be satisfied **before** or **after** wh-movement.

(45) a. DS: $[_{IP}$ Steve$_1$ wondered $[_{CP}$ $[_{IP}$ Ted$_2$ liked [which picture of himself$_{*1/2}$]]]]

b. SS/LF: $[_{IP}$ Steve$_1$ wondered $[_{CP}$ [which picture of himself$_{1/*2}$]$_3$ $[_{IP}$ Ted$_2$ liked t$_3$]]]

Alternatively, however, if (45b) is a well-formed LF and LF reconstruction is optional, the ambiguity of (44) may be resolved at LF: the upstairs reading from (46a) and the downstairs reading from (46b).

(46) a. LF$_1$: $[_{IP}$ Steve wondered $[_{CP}$ [which picture of himself]$_3$ $[_{IP}$ Ted liked t$_3$]]]

b. LF$_2$: $[_{IP}$ Steve wondered $[_{CP}$ [which] $[_{IP}$ Ted liked <<picture of himself>>]]]

To summarize, we may maintain the thesis that anaphors are uniformly licensed at LF.

Finally, let's briefly consider the height effects in binding phenomena, discussed by Lasnik and Saito (1991).

Principle A is satisfied in (47a); the anaphor within the matrix VP adjunct is c-commanded by the subject. It is violated in (47b); the anaphor within the matrix VP adjunct is not c-commanded by the potential antecedent inside the subject.

(47) a. [The men] entertained Kono [during each other's vacations].
SU VP ADJUNCT

b. *[The men's mother] entertained Kono [during each other's vacations].
SU VP ADJUNCT

The following satisfies Principle A, patterning with (47a). Such a pattern suggests that subjects and objects are structurally higher than VP adjuncts at some point of the derivation.

(48) Kono entertained the men [during each other's vacations].
OB VP ADJUNCT

In GB, the LF of (48) is (49). Given this, (48) should be ruled out, contrary to fact. That is, the grammaticality of (48) is unexplained under the standard GB approach.

(49) [PP as a VP adjunct]

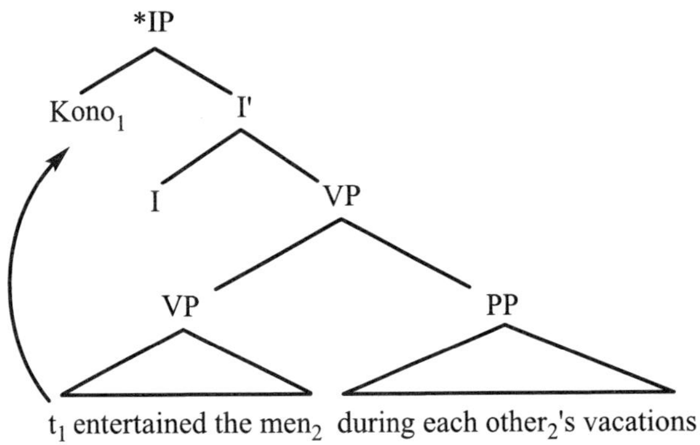

Let's suppose that the object moves **covertly** to a higher position than the VP adjunct at LF. Only then can *the men* bind *each other* in (48).

(50)

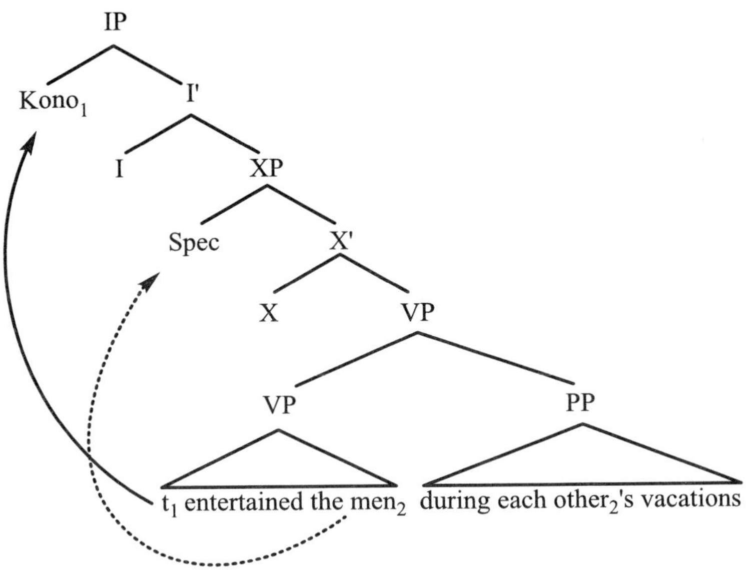

The Case pattern of ECM is parallel to that of normal verbal objects. A GB account of Case assignment cannot explain the paradigm in (51), either.

(51) a. The DA proved [the defendants$_1$ to be guilty] [during each other$_1$'s trials].
EMBEDDED SU — MATRIX VP ADJUNCT

b. *Joan believes him$_1$ to be a genius even more fervently than Bob$_1$'s mother does.

c. The DA proved none of the defendants to be guilty during any of the trials.

In (52a) the embedded subject doesn't c-command the anaphor within the matrix VP adjunct, undesirably causing a Principle A violation. In (52b) the embedded subject pronoun doesn't c-command the R-expression within the matrix VP adjunct. If the sentence doesn't induce a binding problem, it's not clear what causes the ungrammaticality of (52b). Although the NPI within the matrix VP adjunct is not c-commanded by the negative embedded subject in (52c), the sentence is grammatical.

(52) a. The DA $[_{VP}$ $[_{VP}$ proved $[_{IP}$ the defendants$_1$ to be guilty]] $[_{PP}$ during each other$_1$'s trials]].

↑ *C-COMMAND

b. *[Joan $[_{VP}$ $[_{VP}$ believes $[_{IP}$ him$_1$ to be a genius]] $[_{PP}$ even more fervently than Bob$_1$'s mother does]]].

c. [The DA $[_{VP}$ $[_{VP}$ proved $[_{IP}$ none of the defendants to be guilty]] $[_{PP}$ during any of the trials]]].

Let's suppose that the ECMed subject moves to a higher position than the matrix VP adjunct at LF. Only then can *the defendant* bind *each other* in (51a), for example.

9.4 Principle B

According to Principle A and Principle B, anaphors and pronominals should exhibit a complementary distribution. However, they are not always complementary. Complementarity collapses with respect to binding across **DP** boundaries, as follows:

(53) a. They$_1$ never discuss $[_{DP}$ each other's$_1$ work].

b. They$_1$ never discuss $[_{DP}$ their$_1$ work].

(54) a. Every man$_1$ heard $[_{DP}$ a story about himself$_1$].

b. Every man$_1$ heard $[_{DP}$ a story about him$_1$].

(55) a. They$_1$ think that $[_{DP}$ pictures of each other$_1$] are on sale.

b. They$_1$ think that $[_{DP}$ pictures of them$_1$] are on sale.

The above examples indicate that the local domain (or governing category) of Principle A must be different from that of Principle B. If binding domains of Principle A and B were identical, then half of the examples in (53), (54), and (55) would be unacceptable, contrary to fact (cf. Chomsky *KL*).

It seems that Principle B should be computed at DS. In (56) the pronoun *him* cannot be bound by the lower subject *Ted* at DS, as shown in (57). If Principle B applies at SS, *him* cannot refer to the higher subject *Steve*, contrary to fact.

DS (OR LF) EVIDENCE

(56) Steve$_1$ wondered which picture of him$_{1/*2}$ Ted$_2$ liked.

(57) a. DS: [$_{IP}$ Steve$_1$ wondered [$_{CP}$ [$_{IP}$ Ted$_2$ liked [which picture of him$_{1/*2}$]]]]

b. SS: [$_{IP}$ Steve$_1$ wondered [$_{CP}$ [which picture of him$_{*1/2}$]$_3$ [$_{IP}$ Ted$_2$ liked t$_3$]]]

However, if LF construction is possible, it could be concluded that Principle B is computed at LF:

LF EVIDENCE

(58) LF: [$_{IP}$ Steve$_1$ wondered [$_{CP}$ [which] [$_{IP}$ Ted$_2$ liked <<picture of him$_{1/*2}$>>]]]

To summarize, we may maintain the thesis that pronominals are uniformly licensed at LF.

9.5 Principle C

R-expressions, which are non-anaphoric, non-pronominal, and non-pleonastic, cannot be c-commanded by the phrases they are co-indexed with. They must be free in all domains as in (59).

(59) a. *Kono$_1$ voted for Kono$_1$.

b. *He$_1$ expects [$_{CP}$ (that) [$_{IP}$ Kono$_1$ will win]].

c. *Kono$_1$ expects [$_{IP}$ Kamekona to help Kono$_1$].

Co-indexing may be allowed between R-expressions. In (60) there is only one person named *Chin Ho* and the two instances of *Chin Ho* can be co-indexed.

(60) [$_{IP}$ [$_{DP}$ No one who knows Chin Ho$_1$ well] [$_{VP}$ respects Chin Ho$_1$]].

Once a wh-element has moved into Spec of CP, it must not move into an A-position, but only into another Spec of CP. In (61) the second instance of wh-movement is called **improper movement**. If the wh-trace (i.e., variable) in an A-position is bound by the wh-trace in another A-position, the sentence is ruled out due to the violation of Principle C.

(61) *[$_{CP}$ Who$_1$ was [$_{IP}$ t''$_1$ [$_{VP}$ tried [$_{CP}$ t'$_1$ [$_{IP}$ t$_1$ to [$_{VP}$ leave]]]]]]?
A'-POS A-POS A'-POS A-POS

That is, the derivation in (61) is ruled out by the same reason that a pronoun cannot be anaphoric on an R-expression that it c-commands as follows:

(62) *He$_1$ said that Steve$_1$ was brilliant.

Let's compare the following interpretive contrast. (63) is ambiguous, whereas (64) is not.

AMBIGUOUS (63) Who wants me to take him to the concert?

UNAMBIGUOUS (64) Who does he want me to take to the concert?

More precisely, (63) can be interpreted as a question about three different people as in (65a), or as a question about two people as in (65b).

(65) a. [$_{CP}$ Who$_1$ [$_{IP}$ t$_1$ [$_{VP}$ wants [$_{IP}$ me$_2$ to [$_{VP}$ take him$_3$ to the concert]]]]]?
b. [$_{CP}$ Who$_1$ [$_{IP}$ t$_1$ [$_{VP}$ wants [$_{IP}$ me$_2$ to [$_{VP}$ take him$_1$ to the concert]]]]]?

By contrast, (64) doesn't have the reading in (65b). As observed before, this phenomenon is called **Strong Crossover**; wh-movement crossing over a higher co-indexed pronoun is ruled out.

(66) a. [$_{CP}$ Who$_1$ [$_{C}$ does$_4$ [$_{IP}$ he$_3$ t$_4$ [$_{VP}$ want [$_{CP}$ t'$_1$ [$_{IP}$ me$_2$ to [$_{VP}$ take t$_1$ to the concert]]]]]]]?

BOUND R-EXPRESSION

b. *[$_{CP}$ Who$_1$ [$_{C}$ does$_4$ [$_{IP}$ he$_1$ t$_4$ [$_{VP}$ want [$_{CP}$ t'$_1$ [$_{IP}$ me$_2$ to [$_{VP}$ take t$_1$ to the concert]]]]]]]?

As shown in (66b), Strong Crossover can be subsumed by Principle C since the variable (*t_1*) in an A-position is A-bound by the pronoun (*he_1*) in another A-position. In other words, Strong Crossover is a type of improper movement.

In the following, *Steve* must not be bound by either pronoun.

DS EVIDENCE

(67) He$_1$ wondered [which picture of Steve$_{*1/*2}$] he$_2$ liked.

The above example suggests that Principle C should be computed at DS. Allowing Principle C to apply in the course of a derivation does not suffice.

(68) a. DS: [$_{IP}$ he wondered [$_{CP}$ [$_{IP}$ he liked [which picture of Steve]]]]

b. SS: [$_{IP}$ he wondered [$_{CP}$ [which picture of Steve]$_1$ [$_{IP}$ he liked t$_1$]]]

c. LF: [$_{IP}$ he wondered [$_{CP}$ [which] [$_{IP}$ he liked <<picture of Steve>>]]]

(69a) violates Principle C. *To* does not prevent *them* from c-commanding *Steve and Kono*. (69b) observes Principle A and Principle C. How?

(69) a. *It seems [to them$_1$] that Steve and Kono$_1$ were angry.

C-COMMAND

b. Steve and Kono$_1$ seem [to each other$_1$] [t$_1$ to have been angry].

C-COMMAND

The SS and LF of (69b) are given below: Since the reconstruction process in GB is **optional** in the case of A-movement, (70b) **can be** a well-formed LF. Thus, there is no violation of Principle C.

SS (70) a. [$_{IP}$ [Steve and Kono]$_1$ seemed to each other [$_{IP}$ t$_1$ to have been angry]]

LF b. [$_{IP}$ [Steve and Kono]$_1$ seemed to each other [$_{IP}$ t$_1$ to have been angry]]

The contrast between (71a) and (72a) shows that Principle C should not apply at DS. If Principle C applies at DS uniformly, (72a) is predicted to be ungrammatical, contrary to fact.

(71) a. *He$_1$ greeted Kono after Steve$_1$ walked in.

DS/SS/LF b. *he$_1$ [$_{VP}$ greeted Kono [$_{CP}$ after Steve$_1$ walked in]]

(72) a. After Steve$_1$ walked in, he$_1$ greeted Kono.

DS b. *he$_1$ [$_{VP}$ greeted Kono [$_{CP}$ after Steve$_1$ walked in]]

SS/LF c. √[$_{CP}$ after Steve$_1$ walked in]$_2$ [$_{IP}$ he$_1$ [$_{VP}$ greeted Kono t$_2$]]

(73a) violates Principle C at LF after **part of the wh-phrase** in the operator position (e.g., Spec of CP) is **reconstructed** back to its original position, as in (73d). Why is reconstruction optional in (72) but obligatory in (73)?

(73) a. *Which picture of Steve$_1$ did he$_1$ like?

DS b. *he$_1$ did like [which picture of Steve$_1$]

SS c. √[which picture of Steve$_1$]$_2$ [he$_1$ did like t$_2$]

LF d. *which ___ [he$_1$ did like <<picture of Steve$_1$>>]

In GB, there is something like the **Preference Principle**.

(74) The Preference Principle
Try to minimize the restriction in an operator position.

A'-movement involving operators as in (73) must reconstruct if possible. Since A'-movement in (72) is not an instance of operator movement, the reconstruction in (72) is not forced.

To summarize, there were efforts in GB to formulate Binding Theory as **LF** well-formedness conditions via a **reconstruction** process. This LF reconstruction process in GB is totally eliminated in the Minimalist Program once the copy theory of movement is adopted; movement leaves a copy instead of a trace.

9.6 Binding into Complement and Adjunct Clauses

There is a binding asymmetry between (75a) and (75b). The bracketed part in (75a) is a noun-complement clause, and that in (75b) an adjunct clause (i.e., a relative clause).

(75) a. *Which claim [that Steve$_1$ was asleep] did he$_1$ discuss?
b. Which claim [that Steve$_1$ made] did he$_1$ discuss?

The following shows the SSs of (75):

(76) a. which claim that Steve was asleep did [he discuss t]
b. which claim that Steve made did [he discuss t]

The following shows the LFs of (75) after reconstruction:

(77) a. which did [he discuss <<claim that Steve was asleep>>]
b. which did [he discuss <<claim that Steve made>>]

Then, the contrast in (75) cannot be captured.

In this light, Lebeaux (1988) argues that complements **must** be present at DS, but adjuncts **may** be introduced in the course of derivation.

Binding into a noun complement clause has only a single possibility. Since complements are selected by a predicate, they must appear at DS. Given the following derivation, it is correctly predicted that (75a) violates Principle C.

DS (78) a. **he** did discuss [which claim that **Steve** was asleep]
SS b. [which claim that **Steve** asleep]$_1$ did **he** discuss t_1
LF c. *which ___ did [**he** discuss <<claim that **Steve** was asleep>>]

In the case of an adjunct clause, however, there are two possibilities. If the adjunct clause is introduced **before** wh-movement, Principle C is violated, contrary to fact.

DS (79) a. **he** did discuss [which claim that **Steve** made]
SS b. [which claim that **Steve** made]$_1$ did **he** discuss t_1
LF c. *which ___ did [**he** discuss <<claim that **Steve** made>>]

Alternatively, suppose that (75b) has undergone the following derivation: (80a) shows the starting representation of (75b). (80b) shows the SS representation of (75b) after wh-movement. (80c) shows the result of LF reconstruction from (80b). As a next step, suppose that the adjunct clause is introduced as in (80d). Given this scenario, it is correctly predicted that there is no violation of Principle C in (75b).

DS (80) a. he did discuss which claim
SS b. which claim$_1$ did he discuss t_1
LF_1 c. which ___ did [he discuss <<claim>>]
LF_2 d. √which [that **Steve** made] did [**he** discuss <<claim>>]

LATE INSERTION

9.7 Interpretive Binding Theory

On his way to the Minimalist Program, Chomsky (*MP*) proposes the copy (and paste) theory of movement. According to this proposal, an element is assumed to leave behind its copy instead of trace.♣

Traces are syntactic formatives whose structures are frozen. Thus, an syntactic operation cannot peer into the inside of traces. By contrast, since copies have internal structures, an operation may be applicable to part(s) of a copy.

As discussed before, (81a) is subject to Principle B, and (81b) to Principle C.

(81) a. Steve$_1$ wondered which picture of him$_{1/*2}$ Ted$_2$ liked.
b. He$_{1/*2}$ wondered which picture of Steve$_2$ he$_{1/3/*2}$ liked.

Given the copy theory of movement, the SSs of (81) are as follows: < > indicates a copy.

(82) a. [$_{TP}$ Steve wondered [$_{CP}$ which picture of him [$_{TP}$ Ted liked <which picture of him>]]]
b. [$_{TP}$ he wondered [$_{CP}$ which picture of Steve [$_{TP}$ he liked <which picture of Steve>]]]

Since there are multiple copies, some portions of copies are necessarily subject to deletion at both PF (for pronunciation) and LF (for interpretation). Let's focus on LF deletion of copies.

After LF deletion of copies, called **chain reduction**, the well-formed LFs of (81) would be the following:

(83) a. [$_{TP}$ Steve wondered [$_{CP}$ which ~~picture of him~~ [$_{TP}$ Ted liked <~~which~~ picture of him>]]]
b. [$_{TP}$ he wondered [$_{CP}$ which ~~picture of Steve~~ [$_{TP}$ he liked <~~which~~ picture of Steve>]]]

♣ See section 11.2.

The logical forms of (81) are given below:

(84) a. Steve wondered which x Ted liked x picture of him

b. he wondered which x he liked x picture of Steve

Grammar must rule out the unwanted LFs in (85). The question is how.

(85) a. $[_{TP}$ Steve wondered $[_{CP}$ which picture of him $[_{TP}$ Ted liked <~~which picture of him~~>]]]

b. $[_{TP}$ he wondered $[_{CP}$ which picture of Steve $[_{TP}$ he liked <~~which picture of Steve~~>]]]

Chomsky's (*MP*) answer is to use the Preference Principle in (74); the non-quantificational material in the operator position is deleted.

(74) is a **preference** rather than an absolute requirement. If the Preference Principle were an absolute requirement, (86) would not yield binding ambiguity, as shown in (87).

(86) Steve$_1$ wondered which picture of himself$_{1/2}$ Ted$_2$ liked.

(87) a. $[_{TP}$ Steve wondered $[_{CP}$ which picture of himself $[_{TP}$ Ted liked <~~which picture of himself~~>]]]

b. $[_{TP}$ Steve wondered $[_{CP}$ which ~~picture of himself~~ $[_{TP}$ Ted liked <~~which~~ picture of himself>]]]

To summarize, since Principle A is a positive condition, it doesn't have to follow the Preference Principle; i.e., it permits two kinds of chain reductions as in (87). Principle B and Principle C are negative conditions, complying with the Preference Principle.

The following suggests that Principle B should hold at DS:

(88) Kono wondered which picture of him$_{*1}$ Ted$_1$ liked.

The Preference Principle dictates that (89a) is well-formed, and (89b) is not.

(89) a. √$[_{TP}$ Kono wondered $[_{CP}$ which ~~picture of him~~ $[_{TP}$ Ted liked <~~which~~ picture of him>]]]

b. *$[_{TP}$ Kono wondered $[_{CP}$ which picture of him $[_{TP}$ Ted liked <~~which picture of him~~>]]]

Are **indices** true grammatical formatives? Chomsky's (*CT*: 228) answer is negative. Indices violate the Inclusiveness Condition.

(90) The Inclusiveness Condition (Chomsky *CT*)

Computations cannot introduce new elements such as bar levels, indices, or syntactic categories that are not already part of the lexical items computed.

Grammar just associates lexical atoms; it does not create new kinds of formatives. Without indices, the two possible derivations in (89) lead to convergence, and the Preference Principle selects (89a).

In order to eliminate the notion of indices, Chomsky and Lasnik (1995) explore an interpretive version of Binding Theory.

(91) a. Principle A

If α is an anaphor, interpret it as coreferential with a c-commanding phrase in its domain.

b. Principle B

If α is a pronominal, interpret it as disjoint from every c-commanding phrase in its domain.

c. Principle C

If α is an R-expression, interpret it as disjoint from every c-commanding phrase.

For instance, the interpretive Principle B in (91b) would require that *him* in (89a) be interpreted as disjoint from *Ted,*

If indices are not syntactic primitives, Binding Theory should be reformulated as being interpretive.

Exercise 9

《9-1》
What is Strong Crossover? Explain the Strong Crossover effect via Binding Theory. (Do not exceed the length of 20 lines.)

《9-2》
Why doesn't an ovet pronominal anaphor exist? (Do not exceed the length of 10 lines.)

《9-3》
Discuss the derivational account of anaphor binding. (Do not exceed the length of 20 lines.)

《9-4》
Discuss Lasnik and Saito's (1991) height effect in binding phenomena and its theoretical consequence in the P&P model. (Do not exceed the length of 20 lines.)

《9-5》
What is improper movement? Explain it by Binding Theory. (Do not exceed the length of 10 lines.)

《9-6》
What is the Preference Principle with respect to binding? (Do not exceed the length of 10 lines.)

《9-7》
Discuss the Lebeaux effect which shows a binding asymmetry between complement and adjunct clauses. (Do not exceed the length

of 20 lines.)

《9-8》

Discuss the motivation and consequence of the interpretive version of Binding Theory. (Do not exceed the length of 20 lines.)

Luigi Rizzi

http://www.ae-info.org/ae/User/Rizzi_Luigi

- Expertise: Syntactic Theory, Language Acquisition, etc.
- Institutions: University of Siena (since 1995), University of Geneva (1985-1995), MIT (1983-1985)
- Known for: Cartography of Syntactic Structure, Locality, Null Arguments, Parametric Comparative Syntax, Relativized Minimality, etc.

10 Control Theory

Control Theory is concerned with the interpretation of PRO—a covert subject of nonfinite clauses—from a sentence or discourse.

10.1 The PRO Theorem

PRO is a hybrid nominal with both anaphoric and pronominal properties.

(1) PRO: [+anaphor, +pronominal]

In the GB model, *big PRO* refers to a nonovert subject of nonfinite clauses. In (2a), for instance, PRO receives a reference from the controller *Kono*.

(2) a. $Kono_1$ went to the store [$_{CP}$ PRO_1 to buy a book].
b. I_1 want [$_{CP}$ PRO_1 to do well].
c. [$_{CP}$ PRO_1 Running five miles] exhausted me_1.

Arbitrary PRO is used when an nonovert subject does not find an antecedent from adjacent clauses. In this case, PRO has a generic meaning such as *everyone*, *someone*, *anyone*, *one*, or *you*.

(3) a. [$_{CP}$ PRO$_{arb}$ To play ball in the classroom] would be inappropriate.
b. [$_{CP}$ PRO$_{arb}$ Running five miles] is exhausting.
c. [$_{CP}$ PRO$_{arb}$ To be or not to be], that is the question.

In GB, the distribution of PRO is ruled by the **PRO Theorem**.

(4) The PRO Theorem
PRO must be ungoverned.

Nonfinite clauses are always dependent to a main clause with a finite V.

10.2 Nonfinite Clauses

We have two types of obligatory control Vs: subject-control Vs and object-control Vs.

The verb *want* is a subject-control V. In the following, the understood subject PRO refers to the matrix subject.

(5) a. I want to go.
b. I$_1$ want [PRO$_1$ to go].

c.

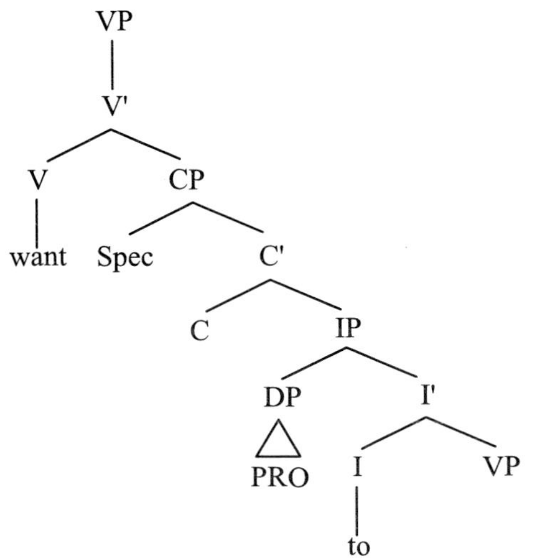

The following illustrates subject-control Vs.

(6) desire, dread, hate, hope, like, love, prefer, promise, wish

The verb *persuade* is an object-control V. In the following, the understood subject PRO refers to the matrix object.

(7) a. I persuaded him to go.

b. I persuaded him_1 [PRO_1 to go].

c.

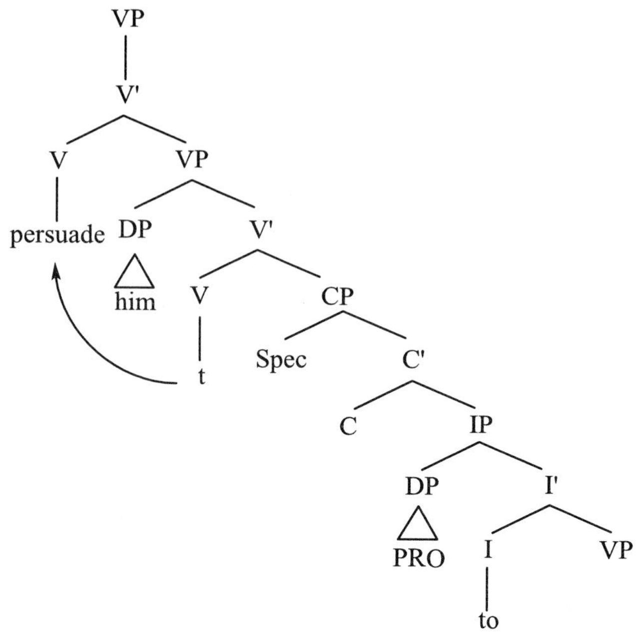

The following illustrates object-control Vs.

(8) advise, allow, ask, beg, cause, coax, convince, dare, encourage, forbid, force, oblige, order, permit, tell

Compare the examples in (9). *Persuade* is a 3-place predicate, and *promise* a 2-place predicate.

MATRIX OB
MATRIX ADJUNCT

(9) a. Steve persuaded Kono to go.
b. Steve promised Kono to go.

What is the GF of *Kono* in each example? As shown in (7b), *Kono* in (9a) plays the role of a matrix object. In (9b) *Kono* is a matrix adjunct.

In (10a) *ask* is an object control V. In (10b) *ask* is a subject control or arbitrary control V.

(10) a. Steve asked the dog_1 [PRO_1 to stop chewing his slipper].

b. $Steve_1$ asked the doctor [how $PRO_{1/arb}$ to stop chewing his slipper].

The verb *expect* was called *Subject-to-Object* (**SO**) ***raising*** V in 1960s. In the following, the DP *him* is raised from the subject position of the lower clause to the object position of the upper clause. The SO raising V is popularly called *Exceptional Case-Marking* (**ECM**) V.

(11) a. I expect him to go.

b. I expect him_1 [t_1 to go].

c.

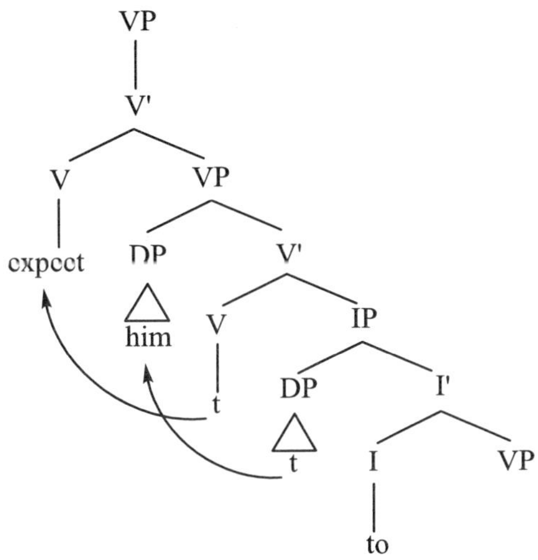

The following illustrates ECM Vs.

(12) assume, believe, consider, find, know, suppose, think, understand

10.3 Distribution of PRO

Why do we need to postulate PRO in nonfinite clauses? One answer is the Extended Projection Principle (**EPP**). The EPP solicits a subject in (14).

(13) The Extended Projection Principle
All clauses must have a subject.

(14) *Arrived a mysterious package.

PRO is the null pronoun subject of only **nonfinite** clauses as in (15). It cannot occupy an object or a subject position of finite clauses. More precisely, (16a) and (16b) violate the PRO Theorem in (4), being governed.

(15) The dog$_1$ tried [PRO$_1$ to chew the slipper].

(16) a. *The dog chewed PRO.
+G

b. *The dog thinks [PRO chewed the slipper].
+G

Both Principle A and Principle B mention the same domain (i.e., governing category). Given this, we deduce the **PRO Theorem** that PRO must be ungoverned. As a consequence, we can further deduce the **PRO Lemma** that PRO must be Caseless, assuming that Case is assigned only under government.

(17) The PRO Lemma
PRO must be Caseless.

The only way for PRO to satisfy the contradictory requirement of Principle A and Principle B is to do it vacuously. If PRO does not have a governing category, Principle A and Principle B will not be applicable.

As shown below, the structural configurations of finite INFL and nonfinite INFL are unvarying. A GB solution is to take advantage of the different feature specifications of INFL. It was thus simply stipulated that the nonfinite INFL is not a governor. Obviously, this is not a genuine explanation.

PROBLEM 1

(18)

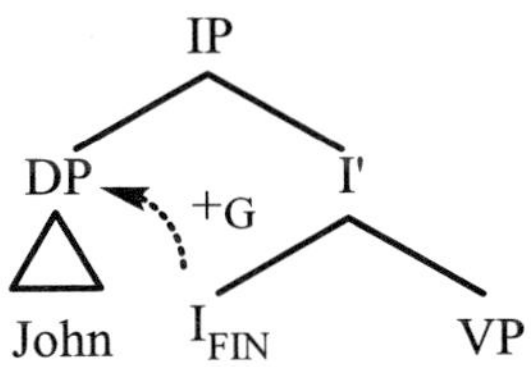

(19)

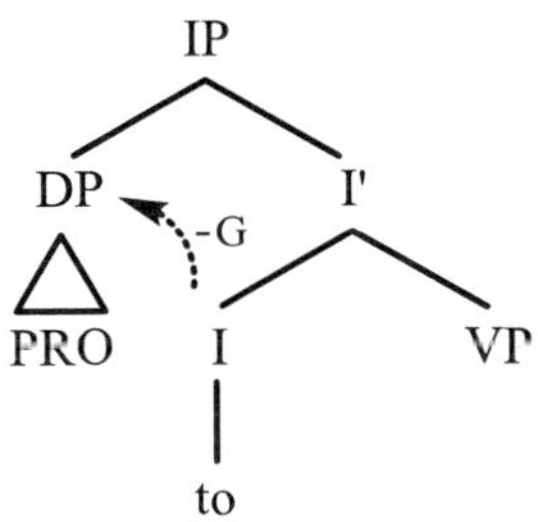

If PRO is not Case-marked, it should violate the **Visibility Condition**:

PROBLEM 2

(20) The Visibility Condition (temporary)
Argument chains must be Case-marked regardless of their phonetic content for them to be θ-marked.

+CASE → +θ

Hence, the Visibility Condition in (20) is forced to be revised as (21). In other words, it amounts to saying that PRO is an exception to the Visibility Condition.

(21) The Visibility Condition (revised)
Only phonetically visible argument chains must be Case-marked for them to be θ-marked.

PROBLEM 3

PRO should move from a governed position to an ungoverned position due to the PRO Theorem. In (22) PRO **was** governed by either the passivized V *elected* or the preposition *to*. A question is then why there is a contrast. This was a puzzle during the era of GB.

(22) a. It is rare [PRO$_1$ to be elected t$_1$ in these circumstances].
-G +G -CASE

b. *It is rare [PRO$_1$ to seem to t$_1$ that the problems are insoluble].
-G +G +CASE

PROPOSAL

Chomsky and Lasnik (1995) propose that PRO receives **null Case** from the nonfinite INFL. Given this proposal, PRO is not an exception to the Visibility Condition. The contrast in (22) is thus explained by Last Resort; movement is prohibited from a Case-marked position to another Case-marked position. (23a) is ruled out in a similar way because *Steve* moves from a Case-marked position to another Case-marked position.

(23) a. *It is rare [for Steve$_1$ to seem to t$_1$ that the problems are insoluble].
+CASE +CASE

b. It is rare [for it to seem to Steve that the problems are insoluble].

CONSEQUENCE

If PRO is Case-marked, we can formulate a government-free approach to Case Theory.

10.4 Movement Theory of Control

Raising and control are apparently similar at their surface forms. It has been one of the issues in the generative tradition how to account for their difference. Consider the following:

(24) a. Kono seemed [to love Adam].

b. Kono decided [to love Adam].

In (24a) the matrix subject *Kono* is thematically related to the nonfinite clause in which it receives θ-role from the embedded verb *love*. As discussed above, this raising construction is derived by A-movement.

(25) Kono$_1$ seemed [t$_1$ to love Adam].

In contrast, the matrix subject in (24b) is thematically related to both the matrix verb (i.e., *decide*) and the embedded verb (i.e., *love*). Since Chomsky (*LGB*), it has been assumed that the embedded clause contains the PRO subject which is controlled by the matrix subject as in (26).

(26) Kono$_1$ decided [PRO$_1$ to love Adam].

The presence of PRO was motivated in Chomsky (*LGB*) by the θ-Criterion at DS, which blocks the movement into a θ-position. However, within the Minimalist Program (Chomsky *MP*, *BPS*, *CT*, *MI*, *DbP*, *BEA*, *TF, UGb, OP*), which postulates only PF and LF levels of representation, thus eliminating DS and SS, the difference between raising and control becomes blurred.

In this light, Hornstein (1999) proposes the movement theory of control, according to which a single DP argument may receive two θ-roles during the derivation, as shown in (27):

(27) Kono$_1$ decided [t$_1$ to love Adam].
↑ +θ ↑ +θ

Given this proposal, obligatory control turns out to be an instance of A-movement. In other words, the mechanism underlying raising and control is non-distinct, except the θ-status of the target position.

As expected, there has been a lot of intense debate about the movement view of control.♣

♣ See Davies and Dubinsky (2004) for recent detailed overviews of the controversy.

Exercise 10

《10-1》

Deduce the PRO Theorem from Binding Theory. (Do not exceed the length of 10 lines.)

《10-2》

Deduce the PRO Lemma from the PRO Theorem. (Do not exceed the length of 10 lines.)

《10-3》

Discuss the motivation for the Null Case approach to PRO. (Do not exceed the length of 20 lines.)

《10-4》

Discuss the motivation for the movement theory of control. (Do not exceed the length of 20 lines.)

11 From GB to Minimalism

Generative Analysis

Minimalism (Chomsky *MP*, *BPS*, *CT*, *MI*, *DbP*, *BEA*, *TF*, *UGb*, *OP*) is the latest ongoing development of an approach to Transformational Generative Grammar.

11.1 Third Factor

Innateness hypothesis postulates **two** distinct **inborn** tools (Chomsky 1975).

(1) a. a **sensory system** for the preliminary analysis of input
 b. Universal Grammar (**UG**)

The main thesis of UG is that the **faculty** of **language** (**FL**) is deep-seated in human mind/brain. The FL is a "system of principles, conditions, and rules that are elements or properties of all human languages not merely by accident but by necessity" (Chomsky 1975: 29).

The overabundance of **grammatical principles** in Principles-and-Parameters (**P&P**) theory called into fundamental questions of how the FL has **evolved** (Chomsky *UGb*).

As acknowledged in Chomsky (*UGb*), dealing with the **diversity** of languages was a big challenge for the P&P accounts of UG. **Minimalism** abandons several pivotal proposals and assumptions of Traditional Generative Grammar. More precisely, Minimalism is concerned with the **FL** in the **narrow** sense (**FLN**), centering on general **computational constraints** rather than narrow grammatical principles.

Regarding human achievements, Chomsky (*Aspects*: 59) states the following:

(2) "However, there is surely no reason today for taking seriously a position that attributes a complex **human achievement** entirely to months (or at most years) of **experience**, rather than to millions of years of **evolution** or to principles of neural organization that may be even more deeply grounded in **physical law**—a position that would, furthermore, yield the conclusion that man is, apparently, unique among animals in the way in which he acquires knowledge."

In later publications, those principles that are grounded in **physical law** turn out to be the **third factor**. As Chomsky (*TF*) observes, there are three factors that might be responsible for the **design** and **acquisition** of language.

(3) a. Genetic endowment
b. Experience
c. Principles not specific to the FL

Genetic endowment, the first factor, sets a limit on the target language, thereby making language acquisition possible. This is the topic of UG. External data are converted to the experience, the second factor, which leads to language variations. Of particular interest is the third of these factors, whose significance is now widely noticed, raising issues about its role in developing the FL. The third factor includes principles of **efficient computation**, which are "of particular significance in determining the nature of attainable languages" (Chomsky *TF*: 6).

The role of the **third factor** in the design and acquisition of language has become immensely stronger, and that of inborn grammatical principles relatively weaker. These developments, however, do not bring theoretical linguistics to an end, just shifting the focus of attention to the third-factor effect.

Chomsky (*TF*: 8) suggests that language acquisition is now "a matter of parameter setting and therefore divorced from the principles of UG" (see also Chomsky *UGb*: 3). In this light, it is necessary to explore the origin of parameters if they do not come from UG. It might be also worthwhile to consider the manner of selecting appropriate parameter values.

Chomsky has more focused on the efficient computation part of the third-factor effects. At least, this is the emerging picture. The rationale behind this is clear as follows:

(4) a. **Minimize experience** because language is more or less **uniform** throughout human species.

b. **Minimize genetic endowment** which only **complicates** the character of the FL. If the FL is to be accounted for in terms of **evolution**, it is better to be the result of a minor change of the mind/brain. The more dramatic that change, the more onerous the task of an evolutionary account in terms of genetic adaptation.

c. It follows that the more we can resort to the third factor, the better for UG and experience. It is desirable for UG and experience to be **slim** and **minimal** as much as possible.

UG doesn't contribute much to our understanding of the many **typological** and **developmental** phenomena for which it previously explained. Almost all of its previous explanatory pressure must be relocated to the other two factors at our disposal—**experience** and **principles not specific to the FL**.

The problem is that we don't know much about the third factor. Chomsky always invokes the vague concept of **evo-devo** [evolutionary-developmental] **revolution** (Chomsky *UGb*: 3).

To summarize, the Minimalist Program is making a **complete change** in the design of the FL. Although a profound explanatory role for **innate domain-specific factors** still remains, there have been efforts to reduce any language-specific innate endowment ideally to a **logical minimum**. We are in the middle of exploring the nature of the third factor.

11.2 What is Minimalism?

There is no unique minimalist theory. We just have a type of the Minimalist Program. **Minimalism** is not a theory so much as a **program** for research. The program has a certain degree of **tentativeness** for implementing leading ideas. It will succeed only if any attempt to execute main ideas contributes to the development of comprehensive analyses and unified theories.

There is a caveat: conducting the Minimalist Program doesn't ensure success. The FL might turn out to be just ugly, inelegant, profligate, unnatural, and massively redundant. If so, the minimalist attempt will meet its Waterloo.

There are two types of economy conditions: methodological economy and substantive economy.

Methodological economy is epitomized as **Occam's Razor** or **Null Hypothesis**:

(5) More is worse, and less is better.

Substantive economy is instantiated as follows:

(6) a. **Shortest Move**: Short hops are preferred over giant leaps.
b. **Last Resort**: Movement must be motivated.
c. **Full Interpretation**: No expressions occur idly in grammatical representations.

We will examine various GB solutions from the perspective of Minimalism. Some solutions will turn out to be on the right track, and others on the wrong track. The Minimalist Program is a tentative project. It is quite imaginable that the FL has **design flaws**. We might reach the conclusion that even the best system cannot avoid some **redundancy** or inelegance. For example, humans have uniformly two **kidneys** and may have up to four **wisdom teeth**. However, one kidney is enough for survival, and wisdom teeth are not used for biting or chewing.

Grammar consists of **representations** (i.e., outputs) and **derivations** (i.e., mapping process). It starts with an abstract structural representation, and changes into another representation by way of structure-dependent **transformations**. The mapping process proceeds until the derivation reaches the final output.

Extra **steps** in derivations and extra **symbols** in representations are excluded by the Economy Principle. The Economy Principle consists of Derivational Economy and Representational Economy. In specific, Representational Economy has its root in Chomsky (*KL*) as the Principle of Full Interpretation, and further developed into the notion of the Bare Output Condition.

(7) a. Principle of Full Interpretation
→ Representational Economy
→ Bare Output Condition
b. Derivational Economy

According to **Representational Economy**, there should be no superfluous symbols in a representation. One candidate is **Full Interpretation**, which states that every element in an expression must receive an interpretation.

According to **Derivational Economy**, there should be no superfluous steps in a derivation. One candidate is **Shortest Move**, which states that economy prefers shorter derivations which make the fewest steps.

In short, **economy** is the **heart** of a minimalist approach to language.

The **computational system** has to interface optimally with other components that impose their own restrictions on the FL. This requirement is called the **Bare Output Condition**. It demands the existence of two interface levels, PF and LF.

Aforementioned, Chomsky (*LGB*) develops **P&P** Theory, which is more popularly called as **GB** Theory. In the generative tradition, Chomsky and Lasnik (1995) reach the climax of GB, and signal the start of Minimalism.

GB has four significant levels of representation: DS, SS, PF, and LF.

(8) **GB** (= EST, T, Y, Inverted Y) **Model**

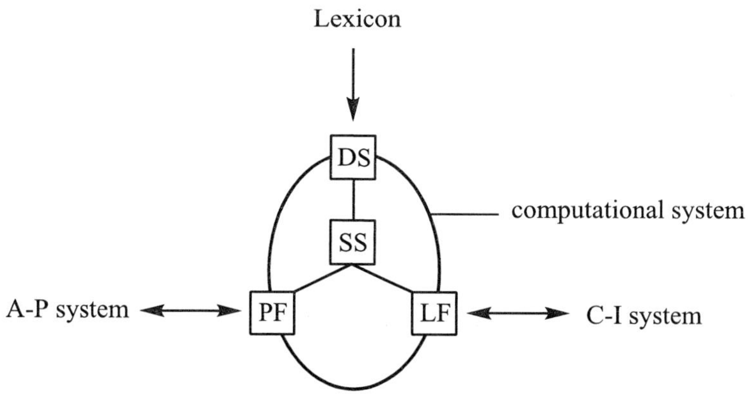

D-structure (**DS**) is the projection of lexical properties, including θ-role assignment and subcategorization. According to Chomsky (*Aspects*), DS is the locus of all lexical insertion as well as being the input to the transformational component.

S-structure (**SS**) is the **enriched DS** derived by transformations, involving traces.

Logical Form (**LF**) is the syntax-semantics **interface** with the Conceptual-Intentional (**C-I**) system of the mind. LF interfaces with a speaker's general knowledge and with extralinguistic cognitive systems.

Phonetic Form (**PF**) is the **interface** with the Articulatory-Perceptual (**A-P**) system. PF is the structure that interfaces with the perceptual system in speech recognition and with the articulatory system in speech production.

The portion of the derivation between DS and SS is called the **Overt Syntax**. The portion of the derivation between SS and LF is called the **Covert Syntax**.

The A-P system and the C-I system are **Performance Systems**, sometimes called as **Grammar-External Systems**.

Classic Minimalism has only two levels of representation: PF and LF.

(9) **Minimalist Model** (*MP, CT*)

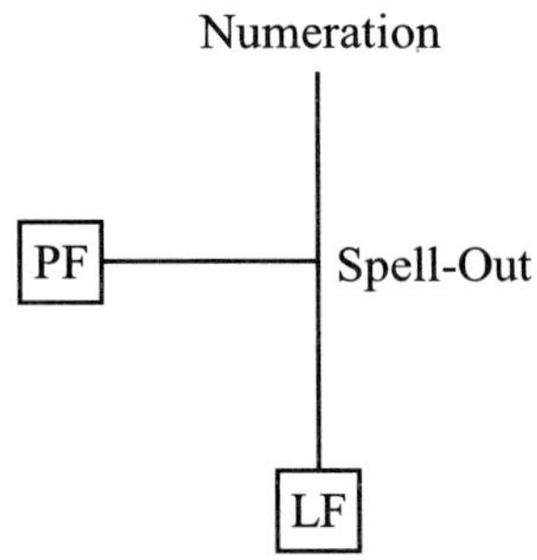

The Strong Minimalist Thesis (**SMT**) contends the following:

(10) Language is an optimal solution to minimal design specifications.

The SMT has following consequences:

(11) There are no superfluous levels: DS and SS are eliminated out of the grammar model. PF and LF are forced by the Bare Output Condition.

(12) There are no uneconomical operations.

(13) There are no superfluous elements such as indices or traces, following the **Inclusiveness** Condition.♣

The **Numeration** is a set of elements selected from the Lexicon and the starting point of the structure building process.

In Chomsky (*MP*), **Spell-Out** is a **point** in the computation of a grammatical representation where the derivation splits and heads toward the two interface levels, PF and LF. Since Chomsky (*BPS*), Spell-Out is an **operation** that takes all phonetic information out of the derivation and ships it to the PF level of representation. After Spell-Out, one representation consists of just phonetic information, and the other everything that is left.

♣ Bare Phrase Structure eliminates categorial distinctions for levels of phrasal projection, thereby conforming to the Inclusiveness Condition (Chomsky *CT*, *MI*), which restricts computations solely to the elements (features) contained in lexical items. Given this condition, computations cannot introduce new elements such as bar levels, indices, or syntactic categories that are not already part of the lexical items computed.

Influenced by Epstein's (1999) and Uriagereka's (1999) independent Multiple Spell-Out (**MSO**) model, Chomsky (*MI*, *DbP*, *BEA, UGb, OP*) revises his (*MP, CT*) former Single Spell-Out model as follows:

(14) **Minimalist Model** in terms of **Cyclic Spell-Out** (*MI*, *DbP*, *BEA, UGb, OP*)

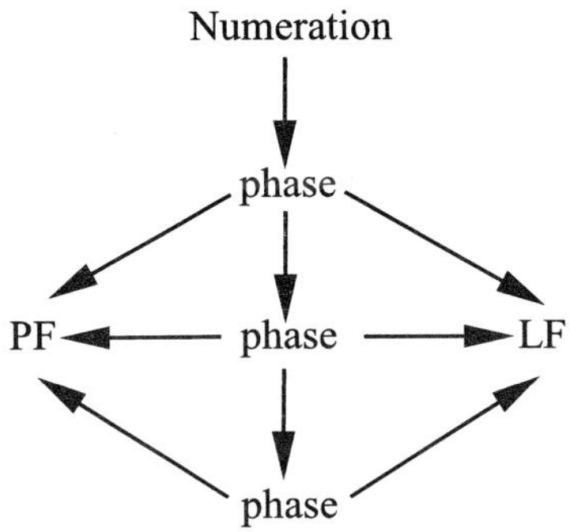

Language combines **sounds** (more generally, gestures, as in sign languages) and **meanings**. Consequently, the interface levels, PF and LF, are ineliminable.

Minimalism maintains the thesis that PF and LF are only levels of representation. Every rule or principle applies either at PF or LF, or at every step of the derivation. Constituents move only for a reason, in compliance with **Last Resort**.

If a representation at PF or LF conforms to the Principle of Full Interpretation, it **converges** at that level of representation. A whole derivation converges if it converges at both PF and LF. Otherwise, it **crashes**.

In GB, lexical insertion was an all-at-once operation, and there was not so much known about the internal process of how DS was formed. Eliminating DS and SS, on the other hand, Minimalism draws special attention to the **internal working** of structure formation processes.

That is, Minimalism has lexical items **inserted on-line** in the course of the syntactic derivation.

Structure building proceeds with two basic operations: Merge and Move (Chomsky *CT*: 250).

(15) a. **Merge** (= Generalized Transformation = External Merge) is the combinatorial process which forms structures from elements in the Numeration and other **partially built** structures.

b. **Move** (= Singularly Transformation = Internal Merge = Copy + Merge + Delete) is the movement process which plays a role in structure building—e.g., a specifier position will be created as part of the process of moving an element into it.

Merge is **asymmetric**. The output of Merge is either (16a) or (16b).

CF. (30) (16) a. Merge X and Y, and Project X.

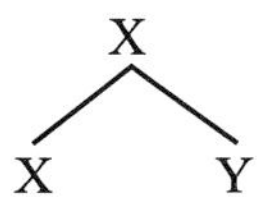

b. Merge X and Y, and Project Y.

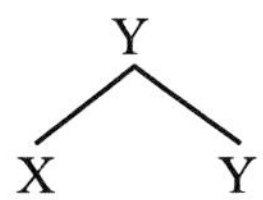

Under the **copy** (and paste) **theory of movement**, Move is a type of Merge.

(17) a. Copy Y.

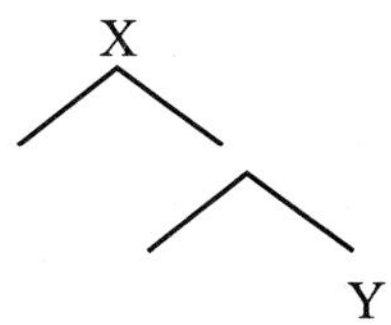

b. Merge Y with X.

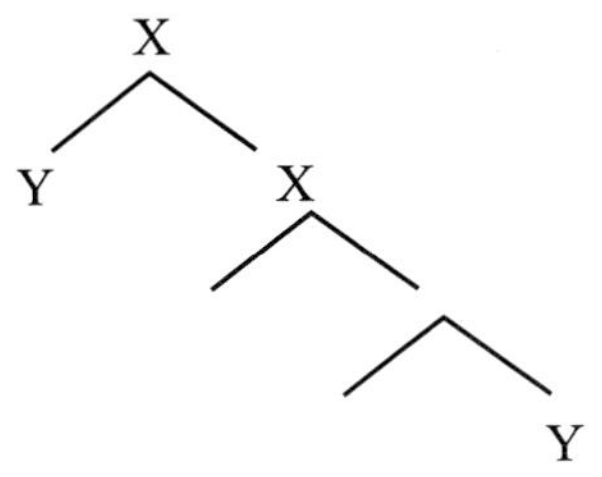

c. Delete lower copy of Y.

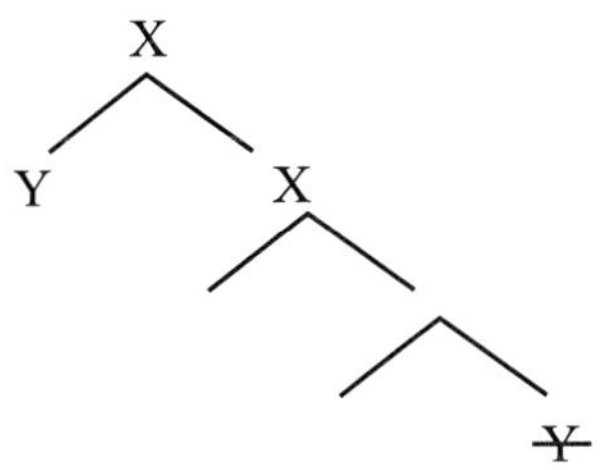

In a trivial sense, **SS** persists in Minimalism as a point called **Spell-Out** (Chomsky *MP*). A question is whether Spell-Out has any of the properties that SS has in GB: Case properties or Binding properties. One of the main goals of Minimalism is to reduce these properties to LF properties, contra Chomsky (*LGB*), as suggested in Chomsky (*KL*).

11.3 Why Minimalism?

From the early 1960s, the central objective of Generative Grammar was to **deduce** general **principles** from various complex **rules** devised for particular languages.

Minimalism keeps sponsoring this project for **simplification**. In particular, it has recourse to ideas such as **Full Interpretation** or **Derivational Economy** from Chomsky's late 1980s paper.

The Principle of Full Interpretation claims that there should be no unwanted elements in the structure of the sentence; each element should play a syntactic, semantic, or phonological role.

(18) Full Interpretation (Chomsky *KL*)
Every element in a sentence must be given an interpretation.

The following violates (18).

(19) *Every the cow chewed the cud.

The Principle of **Economy** is a more general requirement that all **representations** and **derivations** be as economical as possible.

For instance, **Least Effort** and **Last Resort** involve explicit or implicit comparison of derivations. They suggest efforts for the optimal ways of satisfying principles.

As diagrammed in Hornstein et al. (2005: 16), the syntactic objects that A-P and C-I interface systems can read are the subset of all combinations of lexical items that can be constructed by Grammar. From these readable syntactic objects, Minimalism targets only optimally derived ones via comparisons.

(20) a. A shows the objects that are **optimally** constructed and readable by A-P and C-I.
b. B shows the syntactic objects that A-P and C-I can **read**.
c. C shows all combinations of lexical items that Grammar can **construct**.

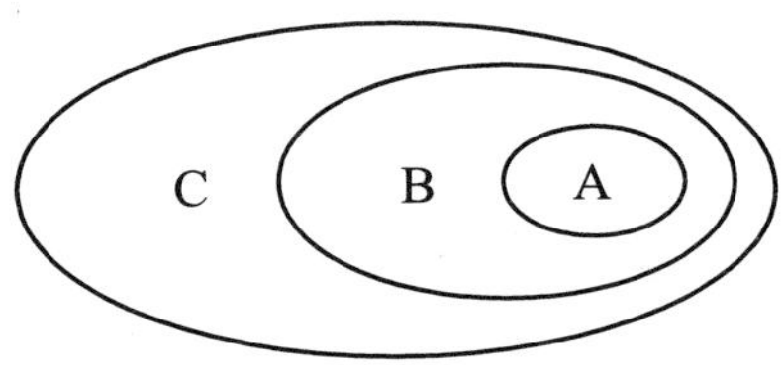

The following cites some criticisms of Minimalism:

(21) "Chomsky's triumphalistic rhetoric is inversely proportional to the actual empirical results that he can point to." (Newmeyer 2003: 586)

(22) "Chomsky's book *The Minimalist Program* is a sad example of spurious science, as it fails to satisfy basic scientific criteria, such as respect for data, unambiguous formulations, falsifiability, and also, on a different level, simple good manners." (Seuren 2004: 4)

Some of Chomsky's responses are given below:

(23) "It is perhaps worth mentioning in this connection that the Minimalist Program, right or wrong, has a certain **therapeutic** value." (Chomsky *CT*)

(24) "One should bear in mind that it is a **program**, not a theory, even less so than the P[&]P approach." (Chomsky *MI*)

(25) "It [*MP*] encourages us to distinguish **genuine** explanations from **engineering** solutions." (Chomsky *MI*)

11.4 Minimalist Design

Minimalism attempts to eliminate the following:

(26) a. DS and SS
b. Government
c. X'

The notion of Government plays a role in the following:

(27)	a.	Case Theory:	Case Government
	b.	Control Theory:	The PRO Theorem
	c.	Government Theory:	The ECP
	d.	Binding Theory:	Governing Category

In GB, nominative Case is assigned by finite INFL to Spec of IP, but accusative Case is assigned by V (or P) to its object. What about ECM? In ECM, accusative Case is assigned by a higher V to the subject of a complement clause.

(28) a. Nom Case, Acc Case

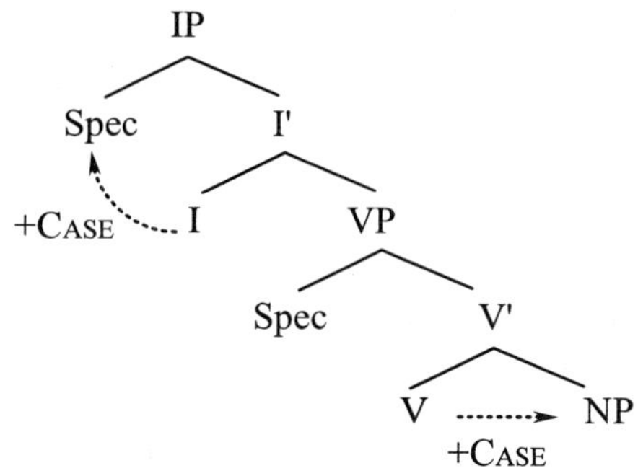

b. ECM: Acc Case

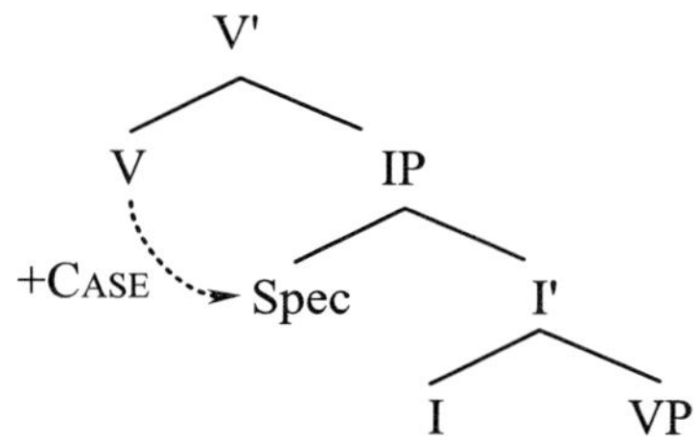

In Minimalism (Chomsky *MP*), there is one general structural configuration under which structural Case is assigned (or checked): the Spec-Head configuration.

(29) a.

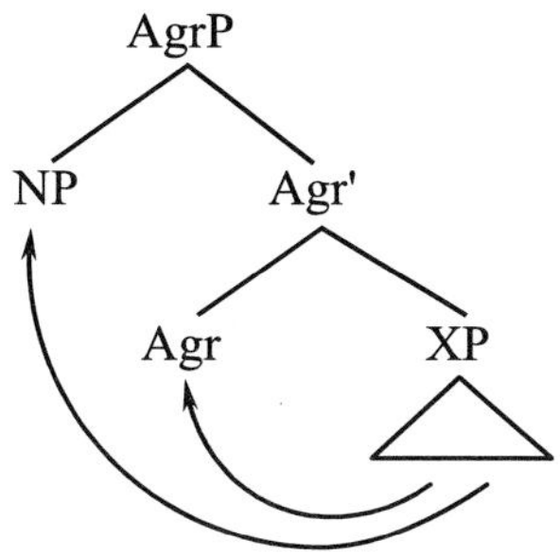

b.

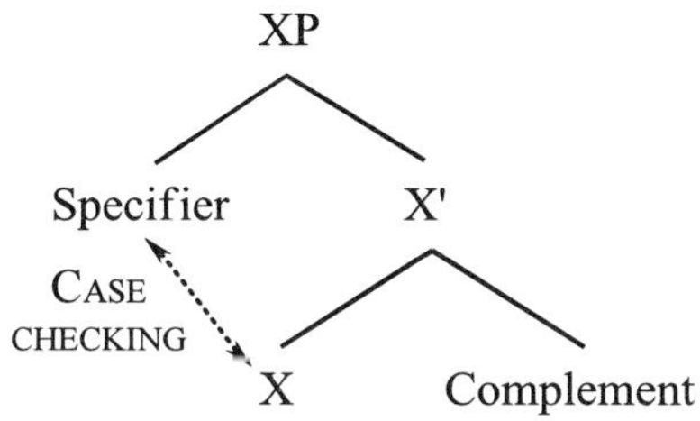

AgrP is a functional category for agreement. AgrSP is a projection for the subject agreement, and AgrOP for the object agreement. Nominative Case is licensed in Spec of AgrSP, and accusative Case in Spec of AgrOP.

X'-structure was fundamental in Chomsky (*LGB, Barriers, MP*), but was replaced with the Bare Phrase Structure since Chomsky (*BPS*).

(30) Merge

K = {γ, {α, β}}, where α, β are objects and γ is the label of K

CF. (16)

X'-theory is not a module of Minimalism. X'-structures follow directly from structure building processes.

(31) a. The combination of two elements forms a binary set, one member of which is the **label** of the set and the other is the set of the two elements combined.

b. {the, {the, dog}}

(32a) illustrates a **top-down** approach to a tree, and (32b) a **bottom-up** approach.

(32) a. X'-tree

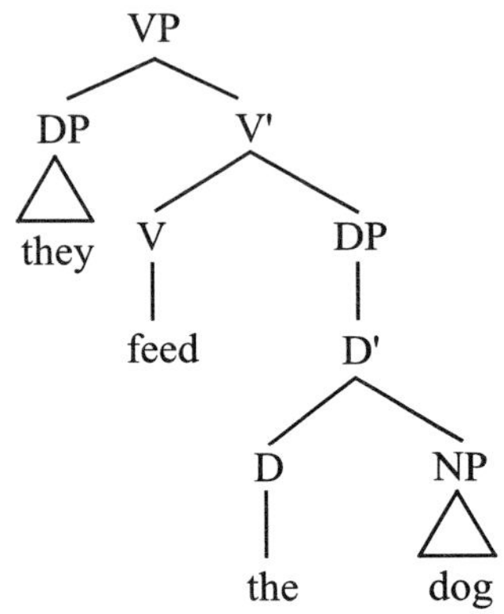

b. Bare Phrase Structure Tree

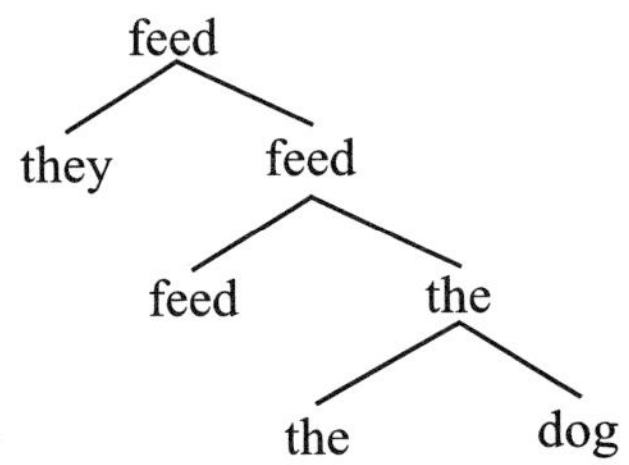

The derivation of (32a) proceeds as follows: VP goes to DP and V'. V' goes to V and DP. DP goes to D and NP via D'. Lexical items are inserted into each terminal node to derive the final string: *They feed the dog.*

The derivation of (32b) proceeds as follows: *the* and *dog* (a label which is a partial tree) merge and project *the* as the label of the first merger. *Feed* and *the* merge and project *feed* as the label of the second merger. *They* and *feed* (a label which is a partial tree) merge and project *feed* as the label of the third merger.

11.5 Principles of Economy

The Principles of **Economy** compare derivations involving the same lexical resources and discard all but the most economical derivations. In the following, therefore, the two sentences are not compared since they start from different numerations:

(33) a. There is a man in the garden.
b. A man is in the garden.

Below, we examine three Economy Principles:

(34) a. Shortest Move (Chomsky *MP*) = The Minimal Link Condition (Chomsky *CT*)
b. Procrastinate
c. Greed

Shortest Move (derived from **Relativized Minimality**) dictates that a constituent move to the first position of the right kind up from the source position. Obeying Shortest Move is regarded as more important than **convergence** at the interface levels.

(35a), violating the Head Movement Constraint (HMC), is ruled out by Shortest Move. (35b), a case of Superraising, **converges**, but violates Shortest Move. (35c), a case of Superiority violation, is ruled out by Shortest Move.

*HMC (35) a. *Have$_1$ Steve will t_1 left by the time we get there?

SUPERRAISING b. *Steve$_1$ is likely for it to seem t_1 to have left.

*SUPERIORITY c. *What$_1$ did you persuade who to buy t_1?

cf. Who$_1$ did you persuade t_1 to buy what?

If you can wait, you must wait. The Principle of **Procrastinate** demands that movement delay until after Spell-Out as long as delay is compatible with convergence. Procrastinate can be violated to insure **convergence**, for instance, when the predicate-internal subject moves to Spec of AgrSP (Chomsky *MP*) or Spec of TP (Chomsky *CT*) before Spell-Out in English.

Procrastinate can be **deduced** from the theory of feature movement (i.e., Move-F or Attract-F). In the covert syntax, only features move. In the overt syntax, feature movement triggers the subsequent pied-piping category movement for PF reasons; scattered features cannot be pronounced. In other words, convert movement is always cheaper than overt movement.

According to **Greed**, movement is motivated for selfish reasons. Greed prevents movement from a Case-checking position to another Case-checking position. It is an instance of Last Resort. The Hyperraising examples in (36) violate Greed.

HYPERRAISING (36) a. *Steve$_1$ seems [t_1 is leaving].
+CASE +CASE

HYPERRAISING b. *Steve$_1$ seems to t_1 [that Danny is leaving].
+CASE +CASE

HYPERRAISING c. *Steve$_1$ was said to t_1 [that Danny is leaving].
+CASE +CASE

The Last Resort of derivational economy has developed as follows:

(37) a. Greed (Chomsky *MP*)

b. Enlightened-Self Interest (Lasnik 1999)

c. Suicidal Greed (Chomsky *CT*)

Let's say that α is a moving element, and β is an element in the target. According to Greed, α moves to β for the benefit of α. According to the Enlightened-Self Interest (ESI), α moves to β for the benefit of either α or β. According to Suicidal Greed (= Attract), β attracts α for the benefit of β.

(38)

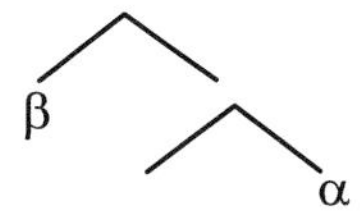

11.6 Derivations and Computations

GB has the starting point of a derivation (i.e., DS). In Minimalism, syntactic structures are built through *Generalized Transformations* (= Merge) that may insert already formed trees (i.e., **partial trees**) into trees.

According to the **Extension Requirement** (Chomsky *MP*), any overt operation on a constituent must expand the constituent structurally in order to create a larger constituent. Head movement prior to Spell-Out causes a small technical problem for a strict interpretation of the requirement that all operations prior to Spell-Out expand the constituent that they target.

As a way out, Chomsky (*MP, CT*) suggests that adjunction before Spell-Out needs not expand a target constituent. Alternatively, Chomsky (*CT*) speculates that head movement may be triggered by PF reasons.

(39) Head Movement

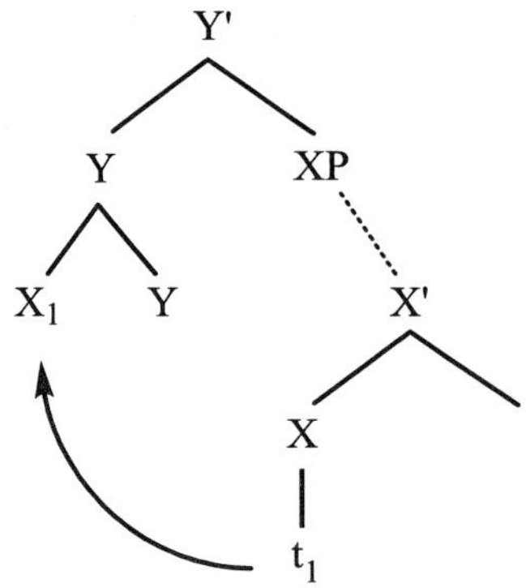

If syntactic operations are confined to the projection and expansion of constituents, derivations will appear to obey a **Strict Cycle Condition**.

11.7 Features and Convergence

Morphological features are features associated with **tense**, **Case**, or **agreement**. They play a role in the **computational system** of language but no role at the PF and LF interfaces.

Lexical items are fully inflected in the Lexicon.

Functional nodes (e.g., Agr or T) serve to carry morphological (inflectional) features necessary to check off the features on Ns and Vs.

Chomsky (*MP*) proposes an extended IP structure: IP = AgrSP + TP. He further assumes that there is a functional category called AgrOP between TP and VP. Recall that AgrSP is a projection for the subject agreement, and AgrOP is a projection for the object agreement. (The solid arrow indicates overt movement, and the dotted one covert movement.)

(40) $[_{CP}$ C $[_{AgrSP}$ AgrS $[_{TP}$ T $[_{AgrOP}$ AgrO $[_{VP}$ SU V OB$]]]]]$

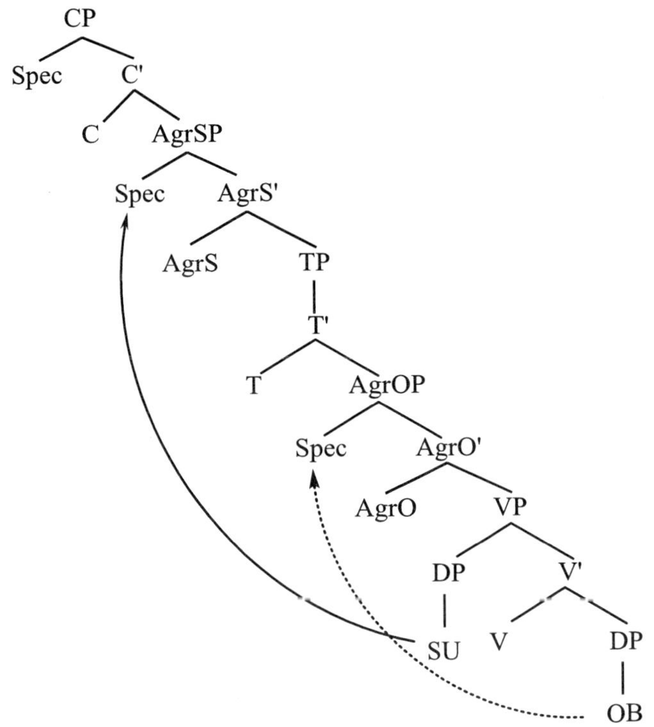

In Lasnik (1999), as in Chomsky (*MP*), it is assumed that AgrO and AgrS are actually the same category, the distinction being somewhat trivial.♣

Chomsky (*CT*) revises (40) as (41). He gives up AgrP (both AgrSP and AgrOP) which is semantically null and void. Instead, he divides verb phrase into vP and VP. v is a light verb which is postulated for transitive Vs or unergative Vs. That is, ergative Vs do not project vP.

♣ A consequence of this is that if the EPP feature resides in AgrS, then it would in AgrO too.

(41) $[_{CP}$ C $[_{TP}$ T $[_{vP}$ SU v $[_{VP}$ V OB$]]]]$

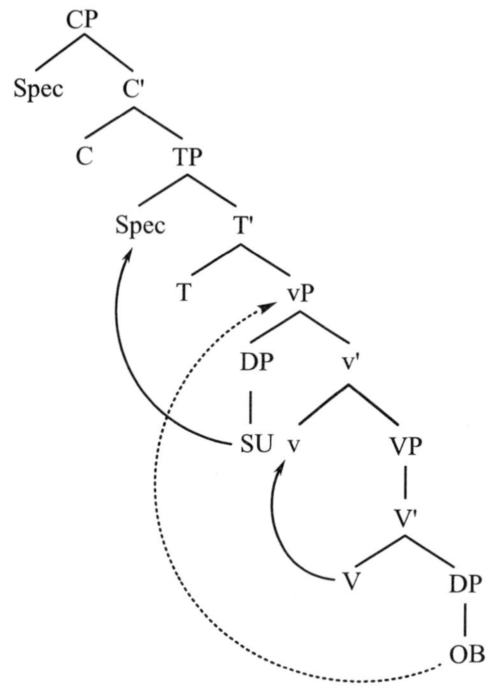

Note that under the Agr-based phrase structure, the object moves covertly to **Spec of AgrOP**. Under the light verb-based phrase structure (and a Multiple Specifier hypothesis), the object moves covertly to the **outer Spec of vP**.♣

Case Theory is reformulated as follows in Minimalism:

(42) a. Nominals must be assigned morphological Case features in the Lexicon before they are inserted into structures via Merge.

b. The Case features on DPs must be checked off during the derivation.

Chomsky (*MP*) assumes that checking occurs only within checking domains. The checking domains of a head H are marked with circles:

♣ The Multiple Specifier Hypothesis permits the recursion of a specifier within one particular projection (e.g., vP or CP).

(43)

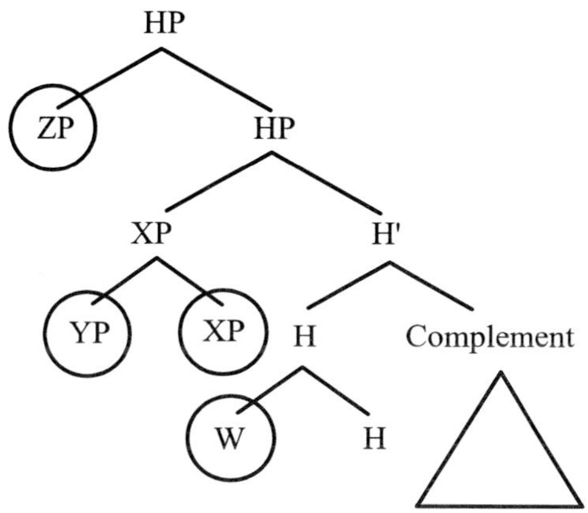

XP, the specifier of a head H, is in the checking domain of H. **YP**, an element adjoined to the specifier XP, is in the checking domain of H. **ZP**, an element adjoined to the maximal projection HP, is in the checking domain of H. **W**, an X-zero element adjoined to the head H, is in the checking domain of H.

The syntactic movement in Classic Minimalism (*MP, BPS, CT*) is triggered by a **feature-driven** operation, which checks off the relevant formal features (**FF**s) of the target heads (e.g., C, T, v) or moving elements.

There are two types of FFs (*CT*): uninterpretable features (e.g., φ-features, Case features, strong/weak categorial features of functional heads) and interpretable features (e.g., categorial features and φ-features of nominals).

In Classic Minimalism (*MP, BPS, CT*), the **strength** of FFs decides whether checking occurs **before** or **after** Spell-Out. If a strong FF is involved, syntactic movement takes place overtly. By contrast, if a weak FF is involved, movement is put off by LF, in compliance with Procrastinate. Chomsky (*CT*) notes that φ-features are likely to be overtly manifested (i.e., have some morphological reflex) when checking is overt. It thus follows that the parametric difference is caused by the relative strength of FFs.

The operation **Move** or **Attract** uses the tool of feature **checking**. On the other hand, the operation **Agree** uses the tool of feature **valuation**. Feature checking in Chomsky (*MP, BPS, CT*) was replaced with feature valuation after Chomsky (*MI*).

Exercise 11

《11-1》
Discuss the three factors that are responsible for the design and acquisition of language. (Do not exceed the length of 10 lines.)

《11-2》
Why is Chomsky's Minimalism a program rather than a theory? (Do not exceed the length of 10 lines.)

《11-3》
What is methodological economy? (Do not exceed the length of 5 lines.)

《11-4》
What is representational economy? (Do not exceed the length of 5 lines.)

《11-5》
What is derivational economy? (Do not exceed the length of 5 lines.)

《11-6》
Explain the architecture of Chomsky's (*MP*) model of grammar. (Do not exceed the length of 10 lines.)

《11-7》
Explain the notion of the Numeration with respect to the Lexicon. (Do not exceed the length of 10 lines.)

《11-8》
Discuss the minimalist history of Spell-Out. (Do not exceed the length of 20 lines.)

《11-9》
Compare Merge with Move. (Do not exceed the length of 10 lines.)

《11-10》
Discuss the consequence of the copy theory of movement. (Do not exceed the length of 10 lines.)

《11-11》
Compare Spell-Out with S-structure. (Do not exceed the length of 10 lines.)

《11-12》
Discuss at least three mechanisms of the P&P model which Minimalism tries to eliminate. (Do not exceed the length of 10 lines.)

《11-13》
Discuss the difference between the top-down approach to phrase structure and the bottom-up approch to phrase strucure, illustrating examples. (Do not exceed the length of 20 lines.)

《11-14》
What is Procrastinate in Chomsky's (*MP, CT*) Minimalim? How can you deduce it? (Do not exceed the length of 10 lines.)

《11-15》
What is the Extension Requirement? (Do not exceed the length of 10 lines.)

《11-16》
Compare Chomsky's (*MP*) Agr-based phrase structure with Chomsky's

(*CT*) light-verb phrase structure, illustrating examples. (Do not exceed the length of 20 lines.)

《11-17》

Discuss the minimalist version of Case Theory. (Do not exceed the length of 20 lines.)

《11-18》

Explain the notion of checking domains. (Do not exceed the length of 10 lines.)

David Pesetsky

http://en.wikipedia.org/wiki/David_Pesetsky

- Expertise: Syntactic Theory, Language Acquisition, Morphology, Russian Syntax, etc.
- Institutions: MIT (since 1988), University of Massachusetts at Amherst (1983-1988), University of Southern California (1982-1983)
- Degrees: MIT (PhD), Yale University (BA in Linguistics)
- Doctoral Advisor: Noam Chomsky
- Dissertation Title: *Paths and Categories* (1982)
- Known for: Comp-Trace Effect, Cyclic Linearization, Earliness Principle, Unselective Binding, Zero Syntax, etc.

12 Phase by Phase

12.1 Cyclic Spell-Out

In Minimalism, DS and SS have been eliminated on the grounds that postulating such internal interface levels is beyond **virtual conceptual necessity**.

With regard to branching to PF and LF, the operation Spell-Out is postulated to apply at an arbitrary point in the derivation, stripping away the features relevant for phonology and sending them off to PF (Chomsky *MP*, *CT*).

As Uriagereka (1999) points out, one **stipulation** in Chomsky's (*MP*) first version of Spell-Out is that Spell-Out applies only once. If **Spell-Out** is an **operation**, Uriagereka reasons that nothing in principle blocks its multiple application in a single derivation, although its application may be subject to economy considerations, i.e., up to **convergence**.

Uriagereka (1999) and Chomsky (*MI*, *DbP, BEA*) propose to dispense with this stipulation by reviving an old idea entertained in the 70s: cyclic access to PF (cf. Bresnan 1971) or to LF (cf. Jackendoff 1972 and Lasnik 1972).

Chomsky (*MI*, *DbP*, *BEA*) suggests that Spell-Out operates iteratively in the course of a derivation, applying as part of the checking of an uninterpretable feature. He suggests that this type of model overcomes a problem with the Single Spell-Out (**SSO**) model noted in Chomsky (*CT*, fn. 50), namely, the fact that uninterpretable features may have a **PF reflex** even when checked and erased in the overt syntax.

The fact that we hear the nominative Case of the embedded subject in (1) is puzzling under the SSO model (Chomsky *MP*, *CT*), since it would mean that the uninterpretable Case feature of *he* can be accessed by the computational system at the point of Spell-Out, although it is already **erased** in the overt syntax.

(1) Kono thinks he left.

The Cyclic Spell-Out (CSO) model offers a solution.

(2) a. [he INFL leave]
→ Spell-Out to PF SO_1 = [he INFL leave]
b. [Kono INFL think SO_1]
→ Spell-Out to PF SO_2 = [Kono INFL think SO_1]

Let's assume that a clause is a cyclic domain, and that the derivation at the end of each cycle automatically sends the relevant phonological information to the PF representation. Given this, the nominative Case of the embedded clause in (1) will be correctly pronounced. If the derivation reaches the matrix clause cycle, another application of Spell-Out will occur.

Is there any way to explain (1) by the SSO model? Maybe. Checked formal features (FFs) are **deleted** but **not erased** for the time being. However, this is obviously a stipulation.

Note the motivation for the CSO model: "Deleted features are literally erased, but **only after** they are sent to the phonological component along with the rest of the structure of Σ—possibly at the **phase** level." In Chomsky (*MI*), different PF outcomes should be **combined**.

In Uriagereka (1999), the Multiple Spell-Out (MSO) operation does not generate overlapping PF outcomes. He explores two approaches to the MSO.

(3) a. Uriagereka I: **Conservative** approach

"Application of Spell-Out to a constituent results in a some kind of "giant lexical compound, whose syntactic terms are obviously interpretable but are not accessible to movement, ellipsis, and so forth."

b. Uriagereka II: **Radical** approach

"Each spelled-out [constituent] actually does not even merge to the rest of the structure, the final process of inter-phrasal association being done in the performative components."

Uriagereka's MSO has an interesting consequence surrounding island phenomena. Consider the following:

(4) a. *What$_1$ did Kono leave the room [$_{island}$ after Danny said t$_1$]? *AC

b. *What$_1$ is [$_{island}$ PRO to park t$_1$ there] illegal? *SC

(4a) violates the Adjunct Condition (**AC**). (4b) violates the Subject Condition (**SC**). Both conditions are generalized into the Condition on Extraction Domains (**CED**) by Huang (1982). The CED is explained by Uriagereka's MSO model. Non-complement domains are **frozen** after both adjuncts and subjects have undergone Spell-Out. That is why extraction out of non-complement domains is not allowed.

Note that Chomsky's (*MI, DbP, BEA*) CSO is a weak version of MSO in the following sense:

(5) The CSO model retains the separate levels of PF and LF.

Epstein et al.'s (1998), Epstein's (1999), Epstein and Seely's (2002, 2006), and Uriagereka's (1999) proposals are strong versions of MSO.

(6) Syntax is maximally dynamic, strongly derivational, not organizing itself in levels of representation, but rather sending information on-line during the course of derivation. Under this view, there are no LF or PF, but rather LF- and PF-**snapshots**, minimal representational unit (called **command units** according to Uriagereka, or **treelets** according to Fodor) which the **performance** systems access and manipulate.

The following is a brief summary of Spell-Out.

(7) a. SSO: Spell-Out applies only once (Chomsky *MP*, *CT*).
b. CSO: Spell-Out applies phase by phase (Chomsky *MI*, *DbP*, *BEA, UGb, OP*).
c. MSO: Spell-Out can apply several times up to convergence (Uriagereka 1999, Epstein 1999).

12.2 Locality

12.2.1 Phases (from *MI* to *OP*)

Some domains are opaque, as observed by Ross (1967).

(8) a. Subjects can move out of a nonfinite clause (IP).
b. Subjects cannot move out of a finite clause (CP).

There have been several approaches to locality.

(9) a. Islands (Ross 1967)
b. Subjacency (Chomsky 1973)
c. Barriers (Chomsky 1986b)
d. Phases (Chomsky 2000)

Syntactic derivations proceed in a **phase** unit with separate lexical arrays. θ-complete **v** and **C** are (strong) phase heads, and T, V, and N are not.

In Chomsky (*MI, DbP, BEA, UGb, OP*), a phase is vP or CP.

(10) a. In Chomsky (*KL*), the Complete Functional Complex (**CFC**) is the semantically well-defined part of a structure.

b. **vP** is a basic proposition which includes a predicate and its arguments.

c. **CP** is an extended proposition which includes vP and all other aspects of meaning (e.g., tense, mood, force).

A-movement cannot cross tensed clauses, but A'-movement can. Spec of CP provides an escape hatch for A'-movement driven by features. The driving feature has been called **P-feature**, **Generalized EPP feature**, or **Edge feature**.

(11) a. P(eripheral)-feature in *MI*

b. Generalized EPP (feature/property) in *DbP* and *BEA*

c. Edge feature in *TF, UGb*, and *OP*

The Phase Impenetrability Condition (**PIC**) motivates cyclic movement.

(12) The Phase Impenetrability Condition (Chomsky *MI*: 108): In phase α with head H, the domain of H is not accessible to operations outside α, only H and its edge are accessible to such operations.

(13)

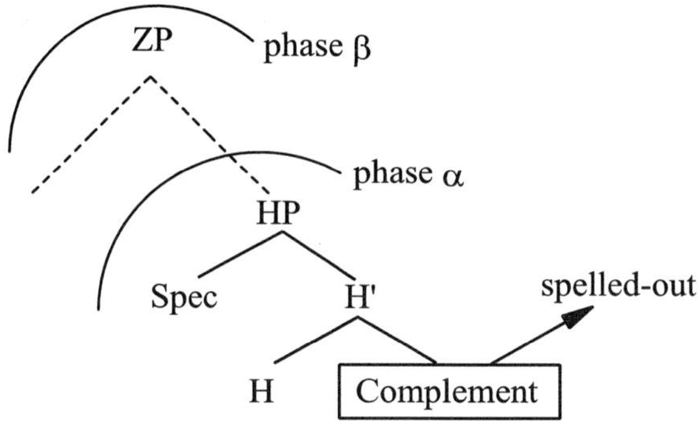

As an illustration of **phase domains** vs. **spelled-out domains**, consider the following:

(14) Danny might think that Steve will fire Kono.

Regarding (14), the first phase is the embedded vP. The first spelled-out material is <fire, Kono>, which is the complement of the phase head v.

(15)

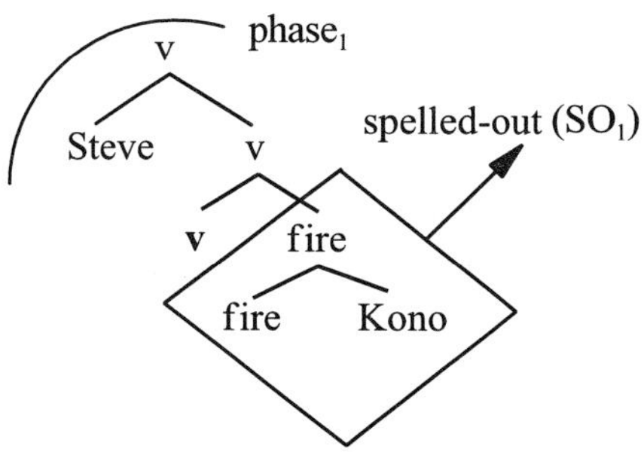

Regarding (14), the second phase is the embedded CP. The second spelled-out material is <Steve, will, ~~Steve~~, v>, which belongs to the complement domain of the phrase head C. <fire, Kono> were already spelled-out.

(16)

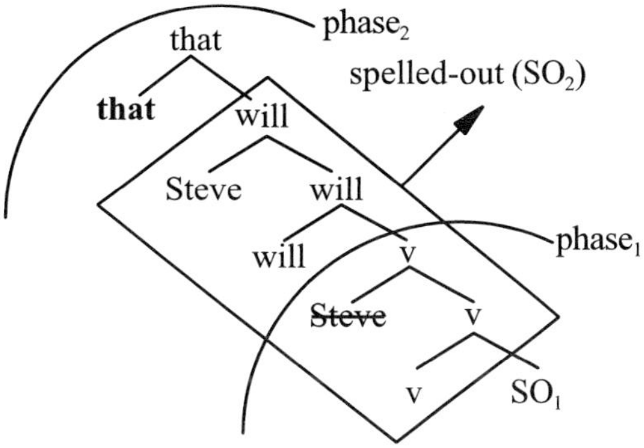

Regarding (14), the third phase is the matrix vP. The third spelled-out material is <think, that>, which belongs to the complement domain of the phase head v. <Steve, will, v, fire, Kono> were already spelled-out.

(17)

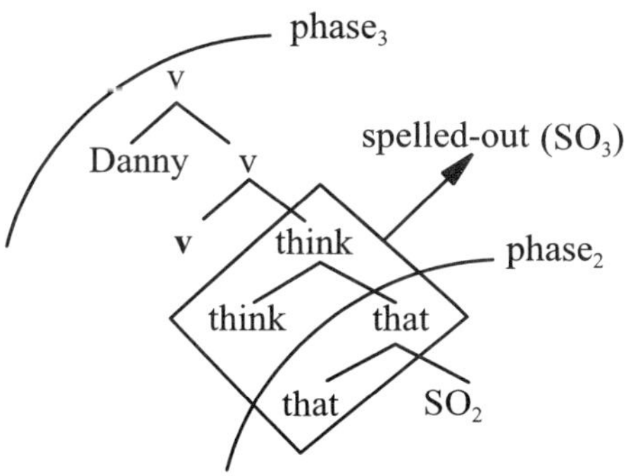

Regarding (14), the final phase is the matrix CP. The final spelled-out material is <C, Danny, might, ~~Danny~~, v>. <think, that, Steve, will, v, fire, Kono> were already spelled-out.

(18)

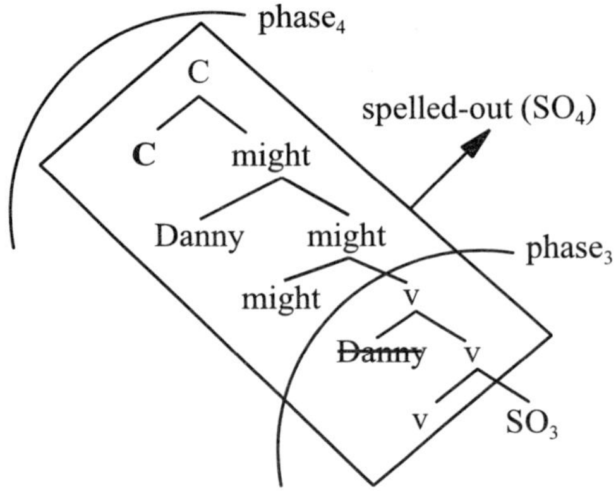

In passive constructions, there is no light v. Consequently, there is only one phase (= CP) in the following:

(19) a. Danny was forgiven.

b. [$_{CP}$ C [$_{IP}$ Danny was [$_{VP}$ forgiven ~~Danny~~]]]
PHASE$_1$

In raising constructions, there is no light v. In the following, there are two phases: phase$_2$ (= CP) and phase$_1$ (= vP).

(20) a. Danny might seem to forgive Steve.

b. [$_{CP}$ C [$_{IP}$ Danny might [$_{VP}$ seem [$_{IP}$ ~~Danny~~ to [$_{vP}$ ~~Danny~~ v
PHASE$_2$ PHASE$_1$
[$_{VP}$ forgive Steve]]]]]]

In the following, there is long-distance wh-movement out of a finite clause. There are four phases for this derivation: phase$_4$ (= matrix CP), phase$_3$ (= matrix vP), phase$_2$ (= embedded CP), and phase$_1$ (= embedded vP).

(21) a. Who did Steve think left?

b. $[_{CP}$ who C (did) $[_{IP}$ Steve I $[_{vP}$ ~~who Steve~~ v $[_{VP}$ think
PHASE$_4$ PHASE$_3$
$[_{CP}$ ~~who~~ C $[_{IP}$ ~~who~~ I $[_{vP}$ ~~who~~ v left]]]]]]
PHASE$_2$ PHASE$_1$

Within the CSO model, the distinction between **pre-Spell-Out** and **post-Spell-Out** movement seems to be blurred. The original distinction between overt and covert movement should collapse once the concept of **phases** is adopted.

Let's briefly check the history of Move. Under the Greed view of Move, movement happens only for the selfish reason of a moving element. There are two executions of Greed. If Move is **category** movement, it is one-step movement. If Move is **feature** movement, it is two-step movement. First, there is Move-F, and then there is ancillary Merge. Under the Attract view of Move, the target attracts features, and then there is ancillary Merge. Under the Agree view of Move, there is no feature movement. After uninterpretable activating features are valued via Agree, the Generalized EPP feature may trigger category movement.

(22) a. Greed: α moves to β for the benefit of α.

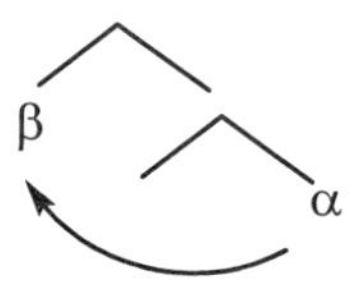

b. Attract: β attracts α for the benefit of β.

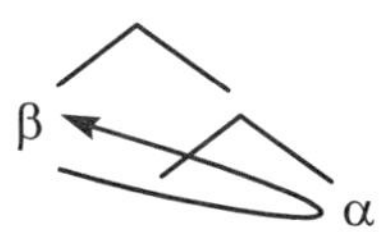

c. Agree: β agrees with α without accompanying actual movement.

(23) a. Move in terms of **Greed**
Move-F + Ancillary Merge (= Pied-piping Move)
b. Move in terms of **Attract**
Attract-F + Ancillary Merge (= Pied-piping Move)
c. Move in terms of **Agree**
Agree + Move

12.2.2 Barriers and Phases

GB approaches to the locality condition on movement assumed intermediate stops between the source position and the target position. As one execution of this idea, Chomsky (*Barriers*) proposes that there may be a barrier between two different syntactic positions of an element. Consider the following:

(24) Who did Steve kiss?

Barriers

(25) $[_{CP}$ who$_1$ did-C $[_{IP}$ Steve$_2$ I $[_{VP}$ t$_1$ $[_{VP}$ t$_2$ kiss t$_1$]]]]

(25) represents a *Barriers*-style derivation of (24). Since VP is a potential barrier, movement crossing over VP induces a locality violation. In order to circumvent this violation, the wh-element (*who*) adjoins to the barrier projection (VP) to nullify the barrierhood.

There is an alternative proposal of circumventing this locality violation. Chomsky (*MI*, *DbP*, *BEA*) proposes that the wh-element in (24) moves to an additional specifier slot of the phase-inducing head, assuming that multiple specifiers are possible. This additional specifier allows a moving element to obviate the potential locality violation.

(26) $[_{CP}$ who$_1$ did-C $[_{TP}$ Steve$_2$ T $[_{vP}$ t$_1$ $[_{vP}$ t$_2$ v $[_{VP}$ kiss t$_1]]]]]$

The relevant bounding nodes are CP and VP in *Barriers*. They are CP and vP in *MI*, *DbP*, *BEA*. IP is defined as a **defective** projection in *Barriers*. It is not an inherent barrier, and can only become an inherited barrier.♣ Similarly, T is not a phase-inducing head in *MI*, *DbP*, *BEA*.

More precisely, Chomsky (*Barriers*) assumed two types of locality conditions: **Barriers** and **Minimality**.

(27) a. There should be no movement crossing over more than one barrier in the spirit of Subjacency.
b. Minimality dictates that a closer governor overrides a potential governor further away.

Minimality was then relativized by Rizzi (1990). **Relativized Minimality** has survived in the tumultuous Minimalism. Indeed, up to *MI*, it seemed to be an only valid condition on locality in various forms.

(28) a. Shortest Move (*MP*)
b. The Minimal Link Condition (*CT*)
c. Attract Closest (*CT*)

The other (more fundamental) locality condition, **barriers**, which was absent in Classic Minimalism such as *MP* and *CT*, resurfaced again as **phases** in *MI*.

To summarize, the two-party locality conditions of Barriers and Minimality conflated into a single condition of Relativized Minimality, which decomposed again by reintroducing bounding nodes in terms of phases (*MI*, *DbP*, *BEA*).

There have been attempts to supplement the stock of barriers or phases. Grammar has room for maneuver: **additional barriers** or

♣ See section 5.3 and section 6.4 for the discussion of barriers.

phases. Chomsky (*DbP*, *BEA*) keeps mentioning in an indirect way that other heads such as D or P may be **phasal** as well.

The original **EPP** (*LGB*), the subject requirement, becomes an unmotivated driving force for (overt) ancillary category movement after Move/Attract or Agree: **Generalized EPP**.

12.2.3 Some Problems with Phases

The notion of phases raises a couple of questions about their identity and properties.

(29) a. Why is CP, but not TP, a phase, considering the clausal character of both CP and TP? Is the so-called *phase by inheritance* (e.g., V, D, or P) possible?

b. Why is only the edge (i.e., a head and its specifier) accessible? Where does the EPP come from?

Chomsky claims that since the head of a phase must be accessible for selection and head movement, its specifier must be accessible too (i.e., the PIC) as in *DbP* and *BEA*.

However, **Bouchard** (2002: 342-343) criticizes the notion of phasehood as follows:

(30) a. If a specifier is accessible because a head must be, the **complement** of the head should be accessible.

b. If a head is accessible due to selection, its complement would be more accessible than its specifier since the complement holds a tighter selection relation with the head than the specifier.

Legate (2003) argues that by the definition of a phase in *MI*, passive and unaccusative VPs should also be phases: reconstruction at the edge of a phase (LF evidence) and phonological isolation (PF evidence). Based on Legate (2002), *DbP* introduces a distinction between a **strong phase** and a **weak phase**, but a weak phase has no effect on C_{HL}.

Bošković (2002) argues that **TP** can be **isolated**, based on Right Node Raising data such as follows. That is, TP could be a phase.

(31) a. Steve believes that and Peter claims that, Kono will get a job.
b. I know when, but I do not know where, Amanda met Steve.

Epstein and Seely (2002, 2006) argue against CSO. CSO is adopted for the rhetoric of the feature distinction between **deletion** vs. **erasure** in Chomsky (*CT*). A derivation must strip away uninterpretable features before it reaches the interfaces. When the derivation goes on, **uninterpretable** features turn out to be **unvalued** features, which should become **valued**. Once they are valued, a question is raised how Spell-Out recognizes that previously unvalued features must be transferred to PF and eliminated from C_{HL}. It seems like **looking-back** is unavoidable in addition to **look-ahead**. This will pose a computational burden to C_{HL}.

Let's summarize the size of phasehood and spelled-out chunks in Chomsky's CSO:

(32)	CP	TP	vP	VP
Phasehood	Y	N	Y	N
SO material	N	Y	N	Y

In conclusion, minimalist formulations of phrase structure offer some new conceptual and empirical insights. However, technical modifications to the phase-based approach may be in order.

12.3 Agree

Chomsky (*CT*) proposes that the **EPP** is related to checking of a

categorial D-feature, which is an **uninterpretable** nominal feature. The D-feature checking can be made either by **raising** a referential subject to Spec of TP as in (33b) or by **merging** an expletive in that position as in (33c).

(33) a. _____ is a man in the garden
b. A man_1 is t_1 in the garden.
c. There is a man in the garden.

Agreement is the phenomenon where relevant elements co-vary in features. It has been argued that the agreement relation between elements is subject to locality. An issue is then what kind of locality is involved in the agreement.

Basically, two approaches are suggested regarding the configuration of agreement.

(34) a. Spec-Head (Chomsky *MP, CT*)
b. Agree (Chomsky *MI, DbP, BEA*)

The evidence for **Agree** comes mostly from English existential constructions and Icelandic nominative object constructions, as illustrated in (35) and (36), respectively.♣ In both cases, the agreeing associate DP arguably did not move overtly to the locus of agreement. It thus makes a challenge for the Spec-Head approach to the agreement phenomenon.

(35) a. *There seems [to be two uninvited guests in the party].
b. There seem [to be two uninvited guests in the party].

(36) a. *Mér virðist [Þeir vera skemmtilegir].
me.Dat seem.3sg they.Nom be interesting
'It seems to me that they are interesting.'
b. Mér virðast [Þeir vera skemmtilegir].
me.Dat seem.3pl they.Nom be interesting

♣ Nominative objects refer to nominative Case-marked elements found in the context of Quirky subject constructions.

In this light, Chomsky (*CT*) tries to simplify the relation of feature checking by feature movement (i.e., Move-F or Attract-F). As an alternative, Chomsky (since *MI*) proposes the **operation Agree** according to which a functional head **Probe** checks its **uninterpretable** feature against a **matching** element **Goal**, which is located in the Probe's search space, i.e., complement domain.

Since Chomsky (*MI*), all instances of Case/φ-features checking have been explained by the Probe-Goal Agree relation.

An independent requirement of the EPP or Edge Feature (EF) can be imposed on phase heads. The satisfaction of this requirement is still made in the Spec-Head configuration, which is an ancillary distinct process from Case/φ-features checking. Crucially, however, the Spec-Head relation is no longer a primary concern for C_{HL}.

Within Chomsky's (*DbP, BEA*) framework, certain elements merge into the syntactic working space with **uninterpretable** features that should be subject to **deletion** prior to reaching the **interfaces** (PF and LF). Deletion of these features is accomplished via the operation **Agree**, which is carried out between a **Probe** P and a **Goal** G. Only those elements with **matching** features for the uninterpretable features of P can have an Agree relation with P. The Probe-Goal dependency operates under the following scenario:

(37) The Probe-Goal Dependency

a. Probe and Goal must be **active** for Agree to apply.

b. Agree divides into **Match** and **Valuation**.

c. Probe must contain a full set of features (i.e., it must be **complete**) to delete uninterpretable formal features of matched Goal. (Chomsky *DbP*: 6)

Uninterpretable features activate syntactic objects for Agree.

(38) The Activity Condition

Uninterpretable morphology renders syntactic objects **active**. **Agree** is parasitic on a **Match** relation: a dependency sensitive to the **type** of features two lexical items share, **not** its **value**.

(39) Match

F_1 and F_2 **match** if they belong to the **same feature class** (e.g., [person], [Case], etc.), independently of value (e.g., 1st vs. 2nd person, nominative vs. accusative, etc.).

Crucially, **Agree** relies on **Match**, but not vice versa. **Valuation** requires **Match**, but not every Match is followed by Valuation. This is workable since, for instance, Match can link two syntactic objects, one of which lacks some of the relevant features for a checking operation to make it, i.e., a **defective** element. Therefore, while an element that is not φ-complete may enter into an Agree relation with another element that carries uninterpretable φ-features, the Agree relation cannot eliminate those features on the probe.

Essentially, Chomsky (*MI*) assumes that an Agree relation between a probe and a goal could be **blocked** by an **intervening inactive** goal; an element becomes inactive after all its features have been **valued**. It amounts to saying that a syntactic object may induce an intervention effect while being inactive.

(40) The Intervention Constraint (cf. Chomsky *MI*: 123)

$\alpha > \beta > \gamma$ (where the relation > designates c-command)

Agree (α, γ) fails when α is a probe and β is a closer matching goal to α than γ is, even if β is inactive due to a prior Agree with some probe.

(41) Inactivity of an XP (Chomsky *DbP*)

An XP that eliminates its uninterpretable features is rendered inactive.

The following illustrates an intervention effect:

(42) a. *It$_1$ seems (that) [t$_1$ is likely [Dexter to have finished his work]]. HYPERRAISING

b. *Dexter$_1$ seems (that) [it is likely [t$_1$ to have finished his work]]. SUPERRAISING

c. It seems (that) [Dexter$_1$ is likely [t$_1$ to have finished his work]]. RAISING

(42a) shows an instance of Hyperraising. The Case of the expletive *it* in (42a) was checked in the embedded finite clause, so it is blocked from raising to the subject position of the matrix finite clause, in the spirit of Last Resort.

(42b) shows an instance of Superraising. The DP subject of the lowest embedded nonfinite clause, *Dexter,* had an unchecked Case feature. Even if the next higher embedded subject DP *it* cannot move after Case checking, it still can block the lowest subject DP *Dexter* from raising. That is, it cannot move across the expletive DP to the matrix subject position. This is expected if some version of **Defective Intervention** like (40) is working. Note that the expletive *it*, even with all of its uninterpretable features eliminated, is still counted as a closer matching goal than the DP *Dexter* from the perspective of the probe in the matrix T. It thus constitutes an intervener and blocks the Agree relation between the matrix T and the lowest subject DP *Dexter.*

(42c) shows an instance of raising. The lowest subject DP *Dexter* is raised to the next higher embedded subject position for Case checking. It is stuck there, following Last Resort. The expletive *it* merges into the matrix subject position, again due to Last Resort.

12.4 Feature-Inheritance

Chomsky (*UGb, OP*) reworks the process of licensing nominative agreement in a particular way.

Under the traditional system, Case/φ-features for the subject-verb agreement are located in T. The subject agrees with T, and receives its nominative Case from T or checks off its nominative Case against the matching feature in T, depending on types of Case Theory. The Spec-Head configuration is crucial.

Recently, however, a number of works (e.g., Carstens 2003, Miyagawa 2004) have argued that this approach might be incorrect. As a radical departure, they argue that the subject-verb agreement should be associated with C rather than T.

More precisely, φ-features and Tense, which were assumed to be associated with T, are derived from C.

(43) a. The phase head C has all the features that T needs.

b. When the phase head C is introduced into the derivation, all the features including φ-features in C are inherited to T.

c. After T receives these features from C, T acts as a probe, searching its domain and agreeing with a relevant goal.

(44)

One of the crucial motivations for the C-to-T feature-inheritance system in Chomsky (*UGb*, *OP*) is that C cannot keep uninterpretable features (uFs) for a derivation to converge. Instead, uFs have to be inherited to T. As a result of the inheritance, T attracts features that it agrees with, whereas C attracts the rest of the features purely by the

EF (i.e., without Agree). The prediction is thus as follows:

(45) C never directly triggers Agree because C lacks uF, given feature-inheritance.

There are two main arguments for feature-inheritance.

First, the **co-occurrence** restriction between T and C suggests the possibility of feature-inheritance (Chomsky *OP*). According to Freidin (2004), **T** manifests basic tense features if and only if it is **selected by C**, setting aside default agreements. Otherwise, T lacks φ-features and basic tense features as in raising or ECM infinitival clauses. It thus seems reasonable to assume that agreement and tense features are associated with C, a phase head.

Second, there are some languages in which the morphology of C is inflected, agreeing with φ-features of the embedded subject. Haegeman (1992) reports that the **C-agreement** in West Flemish distinguishes all person and number combinations. The follows shows that embedded subjects are responsible for the agreement pattern.

(46) C-agreement in West Flemish

a.	K	weten	dan-k	(ik)	goan	wegoan.	C + 1SG
	I	know	that-I	(I)	go	leave	
	'I know that I am going to leave.'						
b.	K	weten	da-j	(gie)	goat	weggoan.	C + 2SG
c.	K	weten	da-se	(zie)	goat	weggoan.	C + 3FSG
d.	K	weten	da-tje	(jij)	goat	weggoan.	C + 3MSG
e.	K	weten	da-me	(wunder)	goan	weggoan.	C + 1PL
f.	K	weten	da-j	(gunder) goat	weggoan.		C + 2PL
g.	K	weten	dan-ze	(zunder) goan	weggoan.		C + 3PL

Given the feature-inheritance proposal, let's consider the following example:

(47) a. Who do you think [bought the book]?

b. $[_{CP}$ who$_{[i\varphi,\ uCase,\ Q]}$ C $[_{TP}$ <who>$_{[i\varphi,\ uCase,\ Q]}$ T$_{[u\varphi]}$ $[_{vP}$ <who>$_{[i\varphi,\ uCase,\ Q]}$ bought the book]]]

The wh-phrase *who* in (47) has nominative Case. In the embedded CP clause, all uninterpretable features in C are inherited to T. Since the T head with inherited features has an uninterpretable feature [uφ], it probes its domain and agrees with the suitable goal *who* in Spec of vP. Since the wh-phrase *who* in Spec of vP has an interpretable feature [iφ], [uφ] in T is valued after Agree. As the result of the φ-agreement, [uCase] in Spec of vP is also valued as nominative Case. After the φ-agreement, each EF in T and C **simultaneously** attracts the wh-phrase in Spec of vP to both Spec of TP and Spec of CP.

According to Richards (2007), feature-inheritance should be postulated in the computational system (C_{HL}) in order to distinguish valued uninterpretable features (uFs) and inherent interpretable features (iFs) at the interface levels. Suppose that some **valued uFs** are transferred to the interface at the certain phase level. These features could not be distinguished from **inherent iFs** at that point. Hence, valued uFs must be deleted as soon as possible when features are transferred to the interface. Without feature-inheritance, some valued uFs in C remain undeleted. It is then likely that C_{HL} could not distinguish those features from other iFs at the next phase level. Consequently, the derivation would crash.

If feature-inheritance is operative at the phase level, it follows that C does not have any features after all features including valued uFs in C are inherited to T. All the features in T are deleted at the same time when the Transfer operation occurs.

In other words, the role of T (and also V) has fundamentally changed since Chomsky (*OP*): T does not bear φ-features inherently, but rather inherits them from C.♣ Consequently, T cannot operate as a probe until C is introduced into the derivation. This shift of uFs from C to T makes it possible to distinguish the finite/control T from the raising T in a nonlexical way.♣♣

(48) a. Steve seized the fugitive.

b. Steve $[\text{past}]_T$ seize the fugitive
FINITE

(49) a. Steve tried to seize the fugitive.

b. Steve $[\text{past}]_T$ try [PRO to_T seize the fugitive]
FINITE CONTROL

(50) a. Steve seemed to seize the fugitive.

b. Steve $[\text{past}]_T$ seem [t to_T seize the fugitive]
FINITE RAISING

Since the raising T is not selected by C, it does not inherit φ-features. Lacking φ-features, it thus cannot value Case. That is, the accessibility of C decides the potential of T. Consequently, there is no need to stipulate that the Lexicon contains two different Ts. Rather, the features of the lexical T are decided **functionally** by the distribution of C.

Crucially, under the feature-inheritance proposal, movement to two different specifier positions, Spec of CP and Spec of TP, takes place **simultaneously** and **independently**.♣♣♣ For instance, predicate-internal wh-subjects move directly to Spec of CP without stopping by Spec of TP. More generally, A-movement does not feed A'-movement. This proposal sheds light on the potential of T as a phase head. Phases are only CP and vP, but not TP, in that T lacks the inherent ability to work as a probe by itself.♣♣♣♣

Another question is why a phase head can maintain uninterpretable EF even after feature-inheritance occurs under the Chomsky-Richards

♣
It is assumed that the feature-inheritance proposal applies to v/V, following Chomsky (*UGb, OP*): V inherits its features from v.

♣♣
The control T refers to the nonfinite T in control constructions, and the raising T in raising constructions.

♣♣♣
See Chomsky (*UGb, OP*) for more details.

♣♣♣♣
What about the Extension Condition when *who* moves to Spec of TP from Spec of vP? What about the PF linearization of *who* in Spec of CP and *who* in Spec of TP? That is, how can we linearize the outputs of simultaneous movements of *who* from Spec of vP? What about the Bijection Principle(i.e., a principle stating that an operator must bind one and only one variable)? What is the syntactic status of *who* in Spec of vP after simultaneous movements: DP-t or wh-t, or both?

analysis. Regarding this question, Chomsky (*UGb*: 11, n. 16) answers the following:

(51) "As an uninterpretable feature, EF cannot reach the interface, so presumably deletion of EF is an **automatic** part of the operation of Transfer. Note that the same cannot be assumed for the standard uninterpretable features, which can be deleted only when certain structural conditions are satisfied, and will crash the derivation otherwise."

EF is neither phonological nor semantic. Consequently, regardless of it being valued or unvalued, it should cause crash, but somehow it does not. That is, EF has to vanish upon being satisfied for convergence.

Obata and Epstein (2011) consider the implication of this feature-inheritance proposal. A fundamental question surrounding this proposal is summarized as follows:

(52) How and why do features on C get inherited by T?

Richards (2007) claims that all of the uninterpretable features (except the EF) on C are sent to T as a necessary precondition for convergence. He deduces this from Chomsky's system of **feature-valuation** and the **timing of Transfer**, whereby artifacts produced by C_{HL} are **sent to** the interfaces. According to Richards's argument, **Transfer** (i.e., transfer to the interfaces) and feature valuation must occur simultaneously for convergence. That is, there is no linear ordering between two operations. If Transfer applies **before** feature valuation, uF is sent to the interface **unvalued**, which causes the derivation to crash. If Transfer applies **after** feature valuation, on the other hand, the **distinction** between iFs and syntactically valued uFs disappears from the perspective of Transfer (Chomsky *DbP*, *UGb*). This also leads the derivation to crash because the operation Transfer does not remove now valued uFs from syntactic objects that are sent to the semantic component.

Exercise 12

《12-1》
What is the motivation for the Cyclic Spell-Out model? (Do not exceed the length of 10 lines.)

《12-2》
Compare Uriagereka's Multiple Spell-Out model with Chomsky's Cyclic Spell-Out model. (Do not exceed the length of 20 lines.)

《12-3》
What is the Phase Impenetrability Condition (PIC)? (Do not exceed the length of 10 lines.)

《12-4》
Compare phase domains with spelled-out domains. (Do not exceed the length of 10 lines.)

《12-5》
Discuss the minimalist history of Move: Greed, Attract, and Agree. (Do not exceed the length of 20 lines.)

《12-6》
Compare barriers with phases. (Do not exceed the length of 20 lines.)

《12-7》
Compare the EPP with the Generalized EPP. (Do not exceed the length of 10 lines.)

《12-8》

Discuss Epstein and Seely's (2002, 2006) argument against Chomsky's Cyclic Spell-Out model. (Do not exceed the length of 10 lines.)

《12-9》

Discuss at least two arguements for Agree. (Do not exceed the length of 20 lines.)

《12-10》

Discuss what the Probe-Goal dependency is. (Do not exceed the length of 10 lines.)

《12-11》

What is the Intervention Constraint? (Do not exceed the length of 10 lines.)

《12-12》

What is Feature-Inheritance? (Do not exceed the length of 10 lines.)

《12-13》

Discuss at least two arguments for feature-inheritance. (Do not exceed the length of 20 lines.)

References

Abney, Steven. 1987. *The English noun phrase in its sentential aspect.* Doctoral dissertation, MIT.

Baker, Mark. 1997. Thematic roles and syntactic structure. In *Elements of grammar*, ed. Liliane Haegeman, 73-137. Dordrecht: Kluwer.

Baltin, Mark R. 1987. Do antecedent contained deletions exist? *Linguistic Inquiry* 18, 579-595.

Bošković, Željko. 2002. A-movement and the EPP. *Syntax* 5, 167-218.

Bouchard, Denis. 2002. *Adjectives, number and interfaces: Why languages vary. North-Holland Linguistic Series: Linguistic Variations* 61. Amsterdam: North Holland/ Elsevier.

Bouton, Lawrence P. 1970. *Do so*: *Do* + adverb. In *Studies presented to R. B. Lees by his students*, ed. J. M. Sadock, 17-38. Edmonton: Linguistic Research.

Bresnan, Joan W. 1971. Sentence stress and syntactic transformations. *Language* 47, 257-281.

Burzio, Luigi. 1986. *Italian syntax*. Dordrecht: Reidel.

Carstens, Vicki. 2003. Rethinking complementizer agreement: Agree with a Case-checked goal. *Linguistic Inquiry* 34, 393-412.

Chomsky, Noam. 1957. *Syntactic structures*. The Hague: Mouton.

Chomsky, Noam. 1964. *Current issues in linguistic theory*. The Hague: Mouton.

Chomsky, Noam. 1965. *Aspects of the theory of syntax*. Cambridge, Mass.: MIT Press.

Chomsky, Noam. 1973. Conditions on transformations. In *A festschrift for Morris Halle*, ed. Stephen Anderson and Paul Kiparsky, 232-286. New York: Holt, Rinehart, and Winston.

Chomsky, Noam. 1975. *Reflections on language*. New York: Pantheon.

Chomsky, Noam. 1976. Conditions on rules of grammar. *Linguistic Analysis* 2, 303-351.

Chomsky, Noam. 1981. *Lectures on government and binding*. Dordrecht: Foris.

Chomsky, Noam. 1982. *Some concepts and consequences of the theory of government and binding*. Cambridge, Mass.: MIT Press.

Chomsky, Noam. 1986a. *Knowledge of language: Its nature, origin, and use*. New York: Praeger.

Chomsky, Noam. 1986b. *Barriers*. Cambridge, Mass.: MIT Press.

Chomsky, Noam. 1993. A minimalist program for linguistic theory. In *The view from Building* 20, ed. Ken Hale and Samuel J. Keyser, 1-52. Cambridge, Mass.: MIT Press.

Chomsky, Noam. 1994. *Bare phrase structure. MIT Occasional Papers in Linguistics* 5.

Chomsky, Noam. 1995. Categories and transformations. In *The minimalist program*, 219-394. Cambridge, Mass.: MIT Press.

Chomsky, Noam. 2000. Minimalist inquiries: The framework. In *Step by step: Essays on minimalist syntax in honor of Howard Lasnik*, ed. Roger Martin, David Michaels, and Juan Uriagereka, 89-155. Cambridge, Mass.: MIT Press.

Chomsky, Noam. 2001. Derivation by phase. In *Ken Hale: A life in language*, ed. Michael Kenstowicz, 1-52. Cambridge, Mass.: MIT Press.

Chomsky, Noam. 2004. Beyond explanatory adequacy. In *Structures and beyond: The cartography of syntactic structures* 3, ed. Adriana Belletti, 104-131. Oxford: Oxford University Press.

Chomsky, Noam. 2005. Three factors in language design. *Linguistic Inquiry* 36, 1-22.

Chomsky, Noam. 2007. Approaching UG from below. In *Interfaces + recursion = language?: Chomsky's minimalism and the view from syntax-semantics*, ed. Uli Sauerland and Hans-Martin Gärtner, 1-29. New York: Mouton de Gruyter.

Chomsky, Noam. 2008. On phases. In *Foundational issues in linguistic theory: Essays in honor of Jean-Roger Vergnaud*, ed. R. Freidin, C. P. Otero and M. L. Zubizarreta, 133-166. Cambridge, Mass.: MIT Press.

Chomsky, Noam and Howard Lasnik. 1995. The theory of principles and parameters. In *The minimalist program*, Noam Chomsky, 13-127. Cambridge, Mass.: MIT Press.

Davies, William and Stanley Dubinsky. 2004. *The grammar of raising and control*. London: Blackwell.

Epstein, Samuel David. 1999. Unprincipled syntax and the derivation of syntactic relations. In *Working minimalism*, ed. Samuel David Epstein and Norbert Hornstein, 317-345. Cambridge, Mass.: MIT Press.

Epstein, Samuel David, Erich Groat, Ruriko Kawashima, and Hisatsugu Kitahara. 1998. *A derivational approach to syntactic relations*. Oxford: Oxford University Press.

Epstein, Samuel David and T. Daniel Seely. 2002. Rule applications as cycles in a level-free syntax. In *Derivation and explanation in the minimalist program*, ed. Samuel David Epstein and T. Daniel Seely, 65-89. Oxford: Blackwell Publishers.

Epstein, Samuel David and T. Daniel Seely. 2006. *Transformations and derivations*. Cambridge: Cambridge University Press.

Freidin, Robert. 2004. *Syntactic structures* redux. *Syntax* 7, 100-126.

Haegeman, Liliane. 1992. *Theory and description in generative grammar: A case study in West Flemish*. Cambridge: Cambridge University Press.

Higginbotham, James and Robert May. 1981. Questions, quantifiers and crossing. *The Linguistic Review* 1, 41-80.

Hornstein, Norbert. 1994. An argument for minimalism: The case of antecedent-contained deletion. *Linguistic Inquiry* 25, 455-480.

Hornstein, Norbert. 1999. Movement and control. *Linguistic Inquiry* 30, 69-96.

Hornstein, Norbert, Jairo Nunes, and Kleanthes K. Grohmann. 2005. *Understanding minimalism*. Cambridge: Cambridge University Press.

Huang, C.-T. James. 1982. *Logical relations in Chinese and the theory of grammar*. Doctoral dissertation, MIT.

Jackendoff, Ray. 1972. *Semantic interpretation in generative grammar*. Cambridge, Mass.: MIT Press.

Jaeggli, Osvaldo. 1986. Three issues in the theory of clitics: Case, doubled NPs, and extraction. In *Syntax and Semantics* 19: *The syntax of pronominal clitics*, ed. Hagit Borer, 15-42. Orlando, Flo.: Academic Press.

Kayne, Richard. 1989. Null subjects and clitic climbing. In *The null subject parameter*, ed. Osvaldo Jaeggli and Ken Safir, 239-261. Dordrecht: Reidel.

Kennedy, Christopher. 1997. Antecedent-contained deletion and the syntax of quantification. *Linguistic Inquiry* 28, 662-688.

Kim, Jeong-Seok. 2012. *Syntactic analysis: A first course*. Seoul: Sejin Press.

Kitahara, Hisatsugu. 1993. Raising quantifiers without raising quantifier raising. In *Minimal ideas*, ed. Werner Abraham, Samuel David Epstein, Höskuldur Thráinsson, and C. Jan Wouter Zwart, 189-198. Amsterdam and Philadelphia: John Benjamins.

Larson, Richard. 1988. On the double object construction. *Linguistic Inquiry* 19, 335-391.

Larson, Richard and Robert May. 1990. Antecedent containment or vacuous movement: Reply to Baltin. *Linguistic Inquiry* 21, 103-122.

Lasnik, Howard. 1972. *Analyses of negation in English*. Doctoral dissertation, MIT.

Lasnik, Howard. 1999. *Minimalist analysis*. Malden, Mass.: Blackwell Publishers.

Lasnik, Howard and Mamoru Saito. 1984. On the nature of proper government. *Linguistic Inquiry* 15, 235-289.

Lasnik, Howard and Mamoru Saito. 1991. On the subject of infinitives. In *Proceedings of Papers from the 27th Regional Meeting of the Chicago Linguistic Society*, ed. L. Dobrin, L. Nichols, and R. Rodriguez, 324-343.

Lasnik, Howard and Mamoru Saito. 1992. *Move-α*. Cambridge, Mass.: MIT Press.

Lebeaux, David. 1988. *Language acquisition and the form of the grammar*. Doctoral dissertation, University of Massachusetts, Amherst.

Legate, Julie Anne. 2003. Some interface properties of the phase. *Linguistic Inquiry* 34, 506-516.

May, Robert. 1977. *The grammar of quantification*. Doctoral dissertation, MIT.

May, Robert. 1985. *Logical form: Its structure and derivation.* Cambridge, Mass.: MIT Press.

Miyagawa, Shigeru. 2004. On the EPP. In *Proceedings of the EPP/Phase Workshop*, ed. Martha McGinnis and Norvin Richards. *MIT Working Papers in Linguistics*. Cambridge, Mass.: MITWPL.

Newmeyer, Frederick J. 2003. What can the field of linguistics tell us about the evolution of language? In *Language evolution: The states of the art*, ed. M. H. Christiansen and S. Kirby. Oxford: Oxford University Press.

Obata, Miki and Samuel David Epstein 2011. Feature-splitting internal merge: Improper movement, intervention, and the A/A' distinction. *Syntax* 14, 122-147.

Pesetsky, David. 1982. *Paths and categories*. Doctoral dissertation, MIT.

Postal, Paul. 1971. *Cross-over phenomena*. New York, NY: Holt, Rinehart and Winston.

Reinhart, Tanya. 1995. Interface strategies. *OTS Working Papers in Linguistics*. Universiteit Utrecht.

Richards, Marc. 2007. On feature inheritance: An argument from the Phase Impenetrability Condition. *Linguistic Inquiry* 38, 563-572.

Rizzi, Luigi. 1990. *Relativized minimality*. Cambridge, Mass.: MIT Press.

Ross, John Robert. 1967. *Constraints on variables in syntax*. Doctoral dissertation, MIT.

Seuren, Pieter A. M. 2004. *Chomsky's minimalism*. Oxford: Oxford University Press.

Szabolcsi, Anna. 1997. Strategies for scope taking. In *Ways of scope taking*, ed. Anna Szabolcsi, 109-155. Dordrecht: Kluwer.

Uriagereka, Juan. 1999. Multiple Spell-Out. In *Working minimalism*, ed. Samuel David Epstein and Norbert Hornstein, 251-282. Cambridge, Mass.: MIT Press.

Wyngaerd, Guido Vanden and C. Jan-Wouter Zwart. 1991. Reconstruction and vehicle change. In *Linguistics in Netherlands* 1991, ed. F. Drijkoningen and A. v. Kemenade, 151-160. Amsterdam: John Benjamins.

Index

Occasionally, this book has used the following conventions.

Chomsky (1957)	*SynStrs*
Chomsky (1965)	*Aspects*
Chomsky (1981)	*LGB*
Chomsky (1986a)	*KL*
Chomsky (1986b)	*Barriers*
Chomsky (1993)	*MP*
Chomsky (1994)	*BPS*
Chomsky (1995)	*CT*
Chomsky (2000)	*MI*
Chomsky (2001)	*DbP*
Chomsky (2004)	*BEA*
Chomsky (2005)	*TF*
Chomsky (2007)	*UGb*
Chomsky (2008)	*OP*

Generative Analysis
A Second Course

지은이 | Jeong-Seok Kim

초판 1쇄 인쇄 | 2014년 9월 01일

펴낸곳 | 세진무역
주　소 | 136-034 서울시 성북구 동소문동 4가 278-2 백호빌딩 301호
전　화 | 02-922-2111
팩　스 | 02-922-2113
전자우편 | sejintrc@hanafos.com

가　격 | 18,000원
ISBN 978-89-956507-6-9 (93740)